Explaining the FIRST DECADE of the New Millennium

# THE TEN-YEAR CENTURY

JAMES SUTHERLAND

# THE TEN-YEAR

EXPLAINING THE **FIRST DECADE**

# CENTURY

## OF THE NEW MILLENNIUM

VIKING
Published by Penguin Group
Penguin Young Readers Group, 345 Hudson Street, New York, New York 10014, U.S.A.
Penguin Group (Canada), 90 Eglinton Avenue East, Suite 700, Toronto, Ontario, Canada M4P 2Y3
(a division of Pearson Penguin Canada Inc.)
Penguin Books Ltd, 80 Strand, London WC2R 0RL, England
Penguin Ireland, 25 St Stephen's Green, Dublin 2, Ireland (a division of Penguin Books Ltd)
Penguin Group (Australia), 250 Camberwell Road, Camberwell, Victoria 3124, Australia
(a division of Pearson Australia Group Pty Ltd)
Penguin Books India Pvt Ltd, 11 Community Centre, Panchsheel Park, New Delhi – 110 017, India
Penguin Group (NZ), 67 Apollo Drive, Rosedale, North Shore 0632, New Zealand
(a division of Pearson New Zealand Ltd.)
Penguin Books (South Africa) (Pty) Ltd, 24 Sturdee Avenue, Rosebank, Johannesburg 2196, South Africa

Penguin Books Ltd, Registered Offices: 80 Strand, London WC2R 0RL, England

First published in 2010 by Viking, a division of Penguin Young Readers Group

10 9 8 7 6 5 4 3 2 1



**PHOTO CREDITS: Introduction:** Timothy A. Clary/AFP/Getty Images **13:** Tannen Maury/AFP/Getty Images **22, 23, 100:** AFP/Getty Images **32:** Lyle Owerko/Reportage/Getty Images **41:** Brennan Linsley/AFP/Getty Images **43:** Luke Frazza/AFP/Getty Images **57:** Stephen Jaffe/AFP/Getty Images **58, 126:** Joe Raedle/Getty Images News/Getty Images **64:** Paul Hawthorne/Getty Images Entertainment/Getty Images **73:** Daniel Berehulak/Getty Images News/Getty Images **79:** Marko Georgiev/Getty Images News/Getty Images **83:** Akram Saleh/Getty Images News/Getty Images **85:** Charles Ommanney/Getty Images News/Getty Images **109:** Chip Somodevilla/Getty Images News/Getty Images **115:** Chris McGrath/Getty Images News/Getty Images

LIBRARY OF CONGRESS CATALOGING-IN-PUBLICATION DATA
Sutherland, James, date–
The ten-year century : explaining the first decade of the new
millennium / by James Sutherland.
p. cm.
Includes bibliographical references and index.
ISBN 978-0-670-01223-7 (hardcover)
1. United States—History—21st century—Juvenile literature.
2. United States—Politics and government—2001–2009—Juvenile literature.
3. United States—Politics and government—2009—Juvenile literature.
4. History, Modern—21st century—Juvenile literature. I. Title.
E902.S876 2010 973.93—dc22 2010007314

Manufactured in China Set in Minion Pro Book design by Jim Hoover

*To my son.*
*Thank you for making my life richer. May your decades be even more fascinating than this one. Seize them with both hands, embrace them, and never stop learning.*

# CONTENTS

DISCOVER CARD
HAPPY 2000
NISSIN FOODS
Budweiser
Panasonic
JOE BOXER
JOE BOXER
CBS NEWS
LG
Virgin
ALL STAR CAFE
Kodak
MILLENNIUM GALLERY
MARQUIS

# INTRODUCTION

## *May You Live in Interesting Times*

EVER SINCE THE clock struck midnight and the calendar hit January 1, 2000, it feels like the world has been spinning a little faster. We live in a new era where historical events seem to be a weekly occurrence.

One author has called it "The Age of the Unthinkable." In the *Wall Street Journal*, two historians dubbed the past decade "the Ten-Year Century," arguing that "changes that used to take generations now unfurl in a span of years." A big reason why is technology. Advances in computers and the rise of the Internet have made it much easier to share ideas with other people around the world. Cell phones were already widespread by 2000—but iPods, smartphones, e-readers, and netbooks were all dreams. No one could friend people in other countries on Facebook; no one could freely collaborate by sharing knowledge on Wikipedia.

The biggest effect of this technology is a flood of information. All of this media amplifies the momentous events around us and shapes how we understand them. In fact, this deluge may be one reason why the decade feels so historic. On one hand, the speedy flow of information allows people to react more quickly to events—news sparks more news. On the other hand, all that media noise can make things seem

*On December 31, 1999, Americans and people from around the world gathered in Times Square to celebrate the new millennium, transforming the turn of the century into a wild party.*

more significant than they really are. Certainly there have been historic decades in the past, but most people weren't "eyewitnesses" to that history, watching events unfold on TV or the Internet.

A few decades ago, finding information was a challenge—most Americans were exposed to only a handful of TV news programs, a local newspaper, and maybe a national news magazine. Anything not found there required a trip to the library, and even that would only yield so much information.

Today, filtering out what is important and what is accurate from the barrage of information is the real challenge. And what you choose to pay attention to helps define who you are. Americans today can get their news from only media outlets they agree with, reinforcing their own political views and shielding themselves from exposure to any other views.

The rise of technology has helped create new prosperity, and the spread of ideas and relationships across borders has drawn many people all over the world closer than ever before. There's a greater sense of community on this planet now.

At the same time, it has accentuated differences. As people grow more interconnected, they feel a need to stress the things that make them distinctive—their ethnicity, nationality, or religion. Those contrasts can lead to tension and conflict.

This book explains key moments of the last ten years and how they have transformed both America and the planet—call it a road map for understanding our ten-year century. Obviously it's incomplete. For one thing, it's written from an American viewpoint at a time when global perspective is growing ever more important. It's also a snapshot—we won't fully understand the momentousness of our times for years to come. Some events that seem important to us now will soon be forgotten—and events that receive little attention now will be viewed as historic later.

But I hope this book illuminates some of the themes that have shaped our times. After all, understanding the last ten years will influence how we approach the next ten. And the planet is not showing any signs of slowing down.

# PROLOGUE

## *Hope and Fear*

### PARTY LIKE IT'S 1999

PEOPLE SHOWED UP early for the new century. In New York City's Times Square, a small group of hardy souls camped out days in advance with sleeping bags to have prime spots for the biggest New Year's Eve party in history—the last day of 1999.

It was to be a global celebration. Countries on every continent had planned lavish events, marking the moment the clock struck midnight in each of the world's time zones. But New York City was the heart of the party, and the city reveled in it. The organizers of the celebration there titled it "Times Square 2000: The Global Celebration at the Crossroads of the World."

Crowds started arriving at 6 A.M. on December 31. That was the time the clock hit midnight, January 1, 2000, in the earliest time zone on earth, in the middle of the Pacific Ocean. As the day went on, giant video screens showed festivities in each time zone. In between, more than one thousand musicians, actors, dancers, and puppeteers performed, saluting cultures from around the world. It was a twenty-four-hour, 7-million-dollar marathon of music, fireworks, and confetti.

It felt like most people on the planet wanted to cheer the occasion, to enjoy a time in history when more regions of the world were enjoying peace and prosperity than ever before. Of course the world still faced huge problems, but for many people, this night felt like a celebration. In America, it was a time when the biggest concern on anyone's mind appeared to be whether a computer bug would cause widespread havoc.

There was hope and fear in the air. Hope, because the world seemed to be entering a new age when people could exchange ideas faster than ever, thanks to new technologies like the Internet. Globalization—the phenomenon of increased trade and communication between countries—seemed to be creating new prosperity in many parts of the world. New economic powerhouses, such as India and China, were developing rapidly.

At the same time, the world seemed threatened by new dangers. Terrorism had globalized, too. It had become easier for a few individuals with radical ideas to share knowledge and work together to kill large numbers of people in horrifying attacks. A fresh reminder of this had come two months before the millennium celebrations, when Jordanian intelligence agents had arrested terrorists from a global organization called al Qaeda who were plotting to attack four sites in Jordan that were popular with American tourists, sometime around New Year's Eve.

U.S. intelligence and law enforcement agencies went on high alert, looking for signs that terrorists, possibly from al Qaeda, might try to attack America, too. They got a lucky break. Border authorities stopped an Algerian man trying to cross the U.S.-Canada border in Washington State, who panicked when questioned and tried to run. They arrested him and found a large supply of explosives in his car trunk. Ahmed Ressam was loosely affiliated with al Qaeda and had developed a plot to detonate a powerful bomb at Los Angeles International Airport on New Year's Eve.

Prosperity, technology, improved communications, nationalism, religious extremism, terrorism—all these factors had increased during the late nineties, and they would all play major roles in the coming decade. Globalization promised to bring the people on this planet closer than ever. It also had the potential to allow a few individuals to kill and terrorize people in greater numbers than ever before. This was the hope and fear.

The new millennium was going to be interesting.

# 2000

## *Red America, Blue America*

IN THE YEAR 2000, Hillary Clinton was elected to the U.S. Senate from New York, the first First Lady ever to win elected office. A computer program that allowed people to download songs from the Internet for free, called Napster, became a sensation, and its creators were sued by the music industry for encouraging piracy. Internet service provider America Online bought media empire Time Warner for about $165 billion. A show called *Survivor,* which stranded sixteen people on an island and had them compete to be the last one left, premiered on American television—it was a new format called reality TV.

In 2000, the "Y2K" computer bug proved to be mostly harmless, but the "ILOVEYOU" computer virus spread by email from the Philippines to most of the world, inflicting billions of dollars' worth of damage on computers. Slobodan Milošević resigned as president of Yugoslavia after demonstrators protested his attempt to steal an election. Palestinians and Israelis clashed as Palestinian residents of the occupied territories demanded their own country. America was focused on the closest presidential election in a century.

---

### SO MUCH PROSPERITY

The general feeling in America on January 1, 2000, was optimism. A poll at the time found that 81 percent of Americans were hopeful about what the new century would hold for them and 70 percent were positive about the future of the country. One reason for the optimism was the strength of the American economy. It had been growing since 1991, the longest economic expansion since the country started tracking the figures. Americans were more prosperous than they had ever been.

Another reason was that America faced few obvious military threats, as the earth's lone superpower. From 1945 to 1991, there had been two great powers, the U.S. and the Soviet Union. The countries had dominated world affairs and threatened each other with nuclear weapons. Their ideological struggle, the Cold War, had ended when the Soviet Union collapsed, leaving America as the world's most influential nation. In his State of the Union message in January 2000, President Bill Clinton wasn't exaggerating much when he said, "Never before has our nation enjoyed, at once, so much prosperity and social progress with so little internal crisis and so few external threats."

Globalization and the lowering of economic barriers between countries played a big role in the boom—more trade meant more business and more profits. Technology was another factor—it created new, more efficient ways to do business. For years, measures of worker productivity in the U.S. had grown by an average of 1 percent a year. From 1995 to 1999, productivity grew by almost 3 percent a year. And more productivity led to more profits.

## ELECTION 2K

The continued prosperity was a big source of President Clinton's high popularity ratings. That boded well for Vice President Al Gore, who was running to succeed Clinton in November's election. A majority of Americans wanted a new president who would continue Clinton's economic policies. But American politics wasn't that simple, and the 2000 election ended up being one of the most contested in history. It reflected the increasingly partisan nature of politics in the U.S.—the bitter split between Republicans and Democrats.

For Republicans, the 2000 election was a chance to take back the White House. For Democrats, it was a chance to cement Clinton's legacy and continue his policies for four more years. Vice President Al Gore seemed a good candidate to do that.

Gore had grown up in politics—his father was a senator from Tennessee, and

# PARTISANSHIP

American politics has been partisan since George Washington was president—the two-party system encourages spirited debate over tough issues. But today's politics can be so bitter that the parties find it almost impossible to make compromises for the good of the country. In 2000, this was a problem because, despite the good times, the country was facing tough issues in the future—possible new threats from overseas and the long-term costs of government programs like Social Security and Medicare. The parties were too divided to solve them. Why?

**Safe Seats—**Congressional districts are drawn by state legislators, who tend to create districts with mostly Republican voters or mostly Democratic voters. Better voter data and computer mapping programs were making it increasingly easy to do so. By 2000, few districts were truly up for grabs. The Representatives elected in these "safe" districts tend to be very conservative or very liberal. Their voters don't want them to compromise with the other party.

**Culture Wars—**As voter turnout kept declining in the latter half of the twentieth century, candidates began stressing controversial issues of culture and moral values in elections over "boring" economic and foreign policy issues. These contentious issues, like abortion, same-sex marriage, and gun control, motivate partisan people to vote, but turn off more moderate voters.

**Scandals—**Corruption in politics is not new, but ever since Republican President Richard Nixon resigned in 1974 for abuse of power, politicians have realized they can bring their enemies down by investigating misbehavior. In 1998, it surfaced that President Clinton had had an affair with a White House intern. The Republican majority in the House of Representatives voted to impeach Clinton for perjury and obstruction of justice related to his affair. He was acquitted by the Senate, but the thirteen-month scandal left Republicans and Democrats even more bitterly divided.

Gore followed in his footsteps, winning a Senate seat in 1984. When Clinton chose him as his running mate in 1992, Gore was known as an intelligent politician but not one with the liveliest personality. That didn't matter, because Clinton had personality to spare. Gore was also known as an ethical politician, and that helped the ticket because Clinton already had a reputation for scandals.

In the spring of 2000, Gore quickly clinched the Democratic nomination, but he appeared unsure of how much he should stress Clinton's record during the campaign. On one hand, most voters were satisfied with the direction of the country and wanted to continue Clinton's policies. On the other hand, they did not want four more years of scandals and investigations.

By early 2000, the main Republican challenger to Gore appeared to be another politician's son. George W. Bush was the eldest son of the forty-first president, George H. W. Bush. Just a decade earlier, no one would have predicted that "Dubya"—as people called him because of the Texan pronunciation of his middle initial—would follow in his father's political footsteps. Bush was very loyal to his father, but a different man. He had spent most of his time in the oil business, then worked as general manager for the Texas Rangers baseball team. Bush was also known for drinking too much and sometimes losing his ferocious temper.

But at age forty, Bush had given up drinking and become a born-again Christian. He developed a powerful faith, saying that Jesus Christ had saved him and given his life purpose. And in 1994, he won election as governor of Texas. During the next six years, he gained a reputation for being pragmatic, working with Democrats in the state legislature to pass several key laws. (Of course, many Democrats in the Texas state legislature were more conservative than some Republicans in Congress—Texas is a conservative state.)

Bush's strategy for winning the Republican presidential primaries was simple—appear so unbeatable he would scare away potential challengers. He raised a huge amount of money—so much that five candidates dropped out before the first state party vote for the presidential nominee, the Iowa caucuses. On January 24, he won the caucuses easily. But a week later, Senator John McCain of Arizona trounced Bush in the New Hampshire primary. Bush fought back, however, and won the South Carolina primary. Soon afterward, he locked up the nomination.

Voters had a hard time deciding between Bush and Gore. Bush's chief campaign promise was a $1.3 trillion, across-the-board tax cut for all income groups—an idea that appealed to his conservative base. But he also said he was "a different kind of Republican." The Republican Party had argued for decades that government should not be in the business of aggressively helping people through social programs. Instead, most Republicans believed that if the government allowed the economy to grow, the country would become wealthier and disadvantaged people would benefit from the prosperity. Bush opposed aggressive social programs, but he believed that not everyone was helped by improvements in the economy. Some people got left behind, and he thought government should try to help them, either through limited programs or by aiding charities and religious organizations. He called himself a "compassionate conservative." This appealed to independent voters.

Gore argued that Bush talked about compassion but did not have compassionate proposals. He said Bush's proposed tax cuts would disproportionately favor the wealthiest Americans and leave little money for the supposedly compassionate policies Bush wanted to implement.

Foreign policy was not a major issue in the race. Terrorism did not come up. Gore believed the U.S. could play a role in keeping peace and spreading democracy in the world. Bush argued that the U.S. should focus on its own priorities and not get involved in peacekeeping missions. "I don't think our troops ought to be used for what's called nation-building," Bush said during one debate.

With few issues that excited voters, the media focused mainly on personalities. Gore was perceived by many as a politician, not always genuine or honest, but definitely smart and up to the job. Bush was seen as more likeable, but many questioned whether he was experienced and knowledgeable enough to be president. The impression was reinforced when one TV reporter decided to spring a pop quiz on the Texas governor during an interview, asking him if he knew the name of Pakistan's leader. Bush did not know the answer. (It was Pervez Musharraf.)

As the primary season ended and the campaigns prepared for their summer conventions, many voters were still undecided. Poll numbers swung back and forth several times, but the race seemed to be a virtual tie.

## DOT-COM BUST

For years, the most visible part of the growing economy had been the technology industry, specifically Internet firms. Their success was on display in January, during Super Bowl XXXIV. When TV viewers weren't watching the St. Louis Rams defeat the Tennessee Titans, they watched ads from seventeen different Internet companies or "dot-coms." Those ads cost an average of $2.2 million each for thirty seconds. One firm, with only $5.8 million in its bank account, spent $3.5 million on three ads that night.

In hindsight, the lavish spending by companies that were not yet making any money seems foolish. But at the time everyone assumed that the rules of business were different for the dot-coms. The Internet was an entirely new medium—the first Web page had only been created in 1990. But it was growing rapidly, with millions of new users logging on each year. As new companies (and old ones too) rushed to use the Web to make money, no one knew which companies would succeed.

Investors were willing to put money in dot-coms because they wanted to profit if those companies became success stories. But investors who could usually predict whether traditional companies would make money had little idea about which dot-coms would succeed and which would fail. The founders of Internet companies were idolized as innovators, people with revolutionary ideas who thought outside the box. Many of them were in their twenties or thirties, young computer geeks straight out of college who had never worked in business before.

Most dot-coms raised money by making Initial Public Offerings (IPOs)—they issued stock in the company to investors. This provided cash—the amount depended on what people were willing to pay for the stock. In the past, companies had not usually conducted an IPO until they were already making a steady stream of money. Then the IPO would allow the company to raise cash from investors and use that money to help the company expand its business.

The Internet firms had a different model. The IPO would give them enough cash to operate for a while, even though they were losing money. During that time, they would try to expand their market share—that is, how many consumers used the Web site. The goal was to gain a big enough market share to start making a profit, hopefully before they spent all the money from their IPO.

Investors wanted to own stock of these companies in case they succeeded, so they all rushed to buy the shares when they were issued. That drove the companies' stock prices up. As the prices went up, more and more people started buying the stocks. It became a bubble in the financial market—the more money people made buying and selling Internet stocks, the more money they invested.

Ironically, one of the things that fed the boom was the growth of Internet trading—people could buy and sell stocks online, without talking to a live broker. This accelerated the speed at which people bought and sold shares. Millions of Americans, many of whom had never invested before, bought stocks.

A stock price goes up and down depending on how investors think a company is performing. But as the excitement over the rising prices of Internet stocks grew, the market began to go up and down wildly in ways unrelated to companies' performance. In late 1998, for example, Books-A-Million, a bookstore chain, had announced that it was launching a revamped Web site. It was not big news—other bookstores had far more exciting Web sites. The company stock, which had traded below $5 for a while, shot up 973 percent in just three days. Within a few weeks, it plummeted back down to $15. Millions of dollars changed hands in this frenzy, just one of many during 1998–2000.

By March of 2000, the stock markets had reached all-time highs. But a stock's value is based on what investors think the company is worth. Could the dot-com firms really be worth that much? After all, most were not making a profit yet—they were losing money, and there was no guarantee they would ever make money.

That month, a leading financial magazine published an article with some cold hard facts that answered that question. "When will the Internet Bubble burst? For scores of 'Net upstarts, that unpleasant popping sound is likely to be heard before the end of this year." The article provided evidence that more than fifty of the Internet companies most popular with investors were going to spend all the cash they had before the end of the year. Unless they found a way to become profitable or raise more money, they would be facing bankruptcy.

The Monday after the article appeared, the stock market plunged. And it kept dropping for months. With prices so low, it was impossible for Internet firms to raise more cash. Soon, many went out of business.

There was a lot of finger pointing after the dot-com bubble burst. Many average investors blamed trading firms for not giving them better advice. Some trading firms blamed average investors for not doing their homework. Everyone accused the Internet company founders of being tricksters, selling something that was too good to be true. One journalist later noted, "In retrospect, it seems obvious that money-losing companies created by 26-year-olds should never have been worth billions. But at the time, these companies appeared to have at least a shot at playing extremely important roles in wildly compelling versions of the future."

Despite all the griping, the government did not enact major new regulations to prevent future bubbles. And even though many of the dot-coms went out of business, others did not. Internet retailer Amazon.com soon started making a profit. The auction site eBay continued to be successful. The Internet was not going away.

In fact, new innovators were still emerging. On March 9, a new encyclopedia went online called Nupedia. Less than a year later, its founders would create a side project called Wikipedia. And in September of 2000, the U.S. government approved a patent for a key algorithm used by a young search engine called Google, designed to find pages on the Web more efficiently than other search sites.

## THE ELECTION THAT WOULDN'T END

At one point during the summer of 2000, George Bush led Al Gore by as much as 10 percent in polls. During that time, Bush had accepted the Republican nomination at the Party convention and he had chosen Dick Cheney to be his vice presidential nominee. Most observers thought it a smart pick. Cheney had been a congressman, White House chief of staff for Gerald Ford, and defense secretary for Bush's father. His experience and knowledge shored up Bush's biggest weakness.

Gore had struggled during the summer. Pundits said he had changed messages too many times, and voters just didn't like him. But Gore's poll numbers rose after the Democratic Party convention. There, Gore announced he had selected Connecticut Senator Joe Lieberman to be his running mate. Lieberman was a moderate and the first Jewish vice presidential candidate for a major party. He had a reputation for honesty, unlike Clinton.

*George W. Bush (left) and Al Gore shaking hands at the end of their third presidential debate, in St. Louis on October 17, 2000. It was their final meeting before the election.*

Gore also showed passion at the convention, something he was not known for. When he took the stage to give his address on the final night, after watching a lengthy series of tributes from friends and family and his wife, Tipper, he walked to the podium, wrapped his arms around his wife and gave her a long kiss. It was the first time America had seen the "wooden" politician so human. Gore's message that night and over the next few weeks was that he was a fighter who would take on corporate interests to help the poor and the middle class. A week after the convention, one poll showed Gore leading 47 percent to 46 percent. The race was a virtual dead heat again.

As the polls remained close in the final weeks, the campaigns became more aggressive. Bush's team attacked Gore's honesty. Every statement Gore made was parsed to see if it was 100 percent accurate. Gore had gotten into trouble in the past because some of his statements seemed like exaggerations. It was an effective attack, because if voters believed Gore was dishonest, that undercut his main argument—that he would continue Clinton's policies but not the scandals.

Gore's staff attacked Bush as well. They argued he was too inexperienced to be president, that he had only gotten this far because of his father's influence. Gore's advisers kept asking one question to anyone who would listen: Was Bush ready to lead the country?

On Tuesday, November 7, 2000, voters went to the polls. Popular opinion was still very close; however American presidential elections are decided by the electoral college, not the popular vote. People vote for electors who have pledged to vote for a certain candidate when the college meets. In most states, the winner of the popular vote in that state gets all the electors. So analysts were focused on certain key swing states, especially Florida, Pennsylvania, and Michigan. These had a lot of electoral votes at stake, and polls were close.

Things looked good for Gore early in the evening as polls closed. Exit polls, surveys of voters leaving the polling stations, found the race was close in many key states, but Gore appeared to be ahead. At 7:50 P.M. eastern time, the TV networks called Florida for Gore. Soon, they called Pennsylvania and Michigan in his favor too. Bush had little chance of getting the 270 electoral votes necessary to win.

Bush was having dinner with his family in Austin. His younger brother, Jeb, the governor of Florida, was devastated. They all went home to watch the results in private. But Jeb and Bush's top adviser, Karl Rove, began telling Bush it was not over. Looking at the actual election returns trickling in, they thought the result in Florida was not definite. Sure enough, just before 10 P.M., the networks announced that they had been wrong—Florida was actually too close to call.

Then, at 2:30 A.M., Fox News called Florida for Bush. It now looked like the Texas governor had won the election. Gore called Bush and conceded and headed for a rally to speak to his supporters. But soon his advisers realized that the results were really close in Florida, less than half of 1 percent apart. Under Florida law, if it was that close, the state had to conduct a recount to check the results.

Gore called Bush back. "Let me make sure I understand," Bush said. "You're calling me back to retract your concession." Bush then told Gore that Jeb assured him that he had won Florida. "Your younger brother is not the ultimate authority on this," Gore replied. The election was not over.

## RECOUNT

By dawn Wednesday, no one knew who the next president would be. Gore had an almost 544,000 vote lead in the popular vote, but that mattered little. He had 255 certain electoral votes, Bush had 246. Three states were too close to call. Within a few days, both Oregon and New Mexico's votes went to Gore, giving him 267 votes. Florida would decide the election.

Recounts are not uncommon in U.S. elections. Because mistakes are inevitably made tabulating votes, many states require votes to be recounted if the margin is very small. But it had never been a deciding issue in a modern presidential race. With the stakes so high, the Florida recount became a monthlong political, legal, and public relations battle. Both campaigns immediately sent lawyers and advisers to the state to try to influence the recount process.

The recount fight exposed Americans to a scary fact few had considered before—the methods they used to cast votes were not very accurate. Most states used outdated machines, many with design flaws. Every state and county decided which method to use, and few local governments wanted to invest money in new machines.

The majority of Florida counties used a popular method—punch cards. Voters punched little tabs out on paper cards. The cards were then fed through a scanner that read which tab (or "chad") was punched out and whom the votes were for. But if the chad didn't get punched out all the way, the machine might record that the person voted for no one. Other counties used ballots with design flaws that could lead to some ballots going uncounted. Nationwide, two million ballots were disqualified in 2000 because they registered no vote or multiple votes, according to one study.

The mandatory recount was conducted

by feeding the cards back through the machines. By the time it was done, Bush's lead had narrowed to 930 votes. Gore then asked, as he was entitled to under the law, for a hand recount of votes in some counties. He picked four—Miami-Dade, Broward, Palm Beach, and Volusia—all of which were home to big cities with predominantly Democratic voters. Bush lawyers filed suit in various courts to try and stop the recounts, but county officials began examining ballots where no candidate had been selected, possibly due to an improperly punched chad, trying to see if the machine had rejected the vote wrongly.

The process was time-consuming. Members of each campaign could challenge the election officials' decision on each ballot. Meanwhile, the media broadcast the entire process constantly. Democrats and Republicans went on the air to try to influence the public. The Democrats said Gore just wanted every vote counted. Republicans argued that Gore was trying to change the results. Both claimed the other party was trying to steal the election.

Bush had one big advantage—the Florida state government was controlled by Republicans. His brother was governor, the GOP controlled the legislature, and the top election official, Secretary of State Katherine Harris, had campaigned for Bush. While counties began hand recounts, Harris informed them that she would not extend the November 14 deadline for submitting vote totals to her office.

The counties still hadn't finished by November 26 when Harris certified Bush the winner. Gore appealed to the state supreme court and it ordered a recount of 70,000 ballots the machines had rejected. Bush appealed to the U.S. Supreme Court, which stopped the recount pending a hearing.

On December 11, lawyers for Bush and Gore argued before the nine justices of the U.S. Supreme Court. Bush argued that the Florida Supreme Court had overstepped its authority by ordering the recounts. Gore countered that this was a state issue, and the U.S. Supreme Court had no role.

Supreme Court rulings usually take months, but the justices issued their decision the next day. By a 5–4 vote, they ruled that the recounts should stop. The majority noted that Florida legislators mandated that election results be finalized by December 12. If the state's electoral-college electors were not selected by that date, they could be challenged by members of Congress as illegitimate, which meant Florida might lose its vote entirely. Since the recounts could not be finished by the twelfth, the results had to be accepted as they were. Which meant that Bush won Florida by 537 votes, gaining its 25 electoral votes, putting him over the top at 271 votes. He would be the next president.

## BITTER AFTERTASTE

Gore conceded soon after the Supreme Court's decision. He said it was time for the country to heal. Many called the entire recount process a constitutional crisis. In reality though, while the process was messy, it worked. A new president would take office on January 20, just as the Constitution mandated. In other countries, similar crises have led to soldiers seizing control of the government. But Gore and Bush used lawyers, not tanks, to resolve their dispute.

But the laws governing the entire election and recount process were complex and conflicting. Judges were forced to decide complicated issues rapidly, and even today, scholars cannot agree on what the "right" decision would have been. Unfortunately, that left the judges open to charges that they had ruled based on their own political preferences. All five conservative Supreme Court justices had voted to stop the recount, while all four liberal justices had voted to continue it.

Many Americans knew their country was politically divided, but were shocked to look at the map after the election. There was a stark regional divide between "red America," the states Bush had won, which consisted mainly of the South and the Plains and Rocky Mountain states, plus Indiana, Ohio, Alaska, and New Hampshire, versus "blue America," the states Gore won, which consisted of the Northeast, most of the Midwest, and the Pacific Coast plus Hawaii and New Mexico. (Another sign of the divided electorate—the newly elected U.S. Senate contained fifty Republicans and fifty Democrats. Republican Vice President Cheney would cast tiebreaking votes.)

For Bush, the end of the 2000 election was just the start of his challenges. He had pledged during the campaign to be "a uniter" but was now taking over a country more bitterly divided than before.

# 2001

## *January to September*

AT THE START of 2001, celebrity magazines focused on Sean "Puff Daddy" Combs's breakup with Jennifer Lopez. *Lizzie McGuire* debuted on the Disney Channel. Word leaked out of a new invention called a Segway, which turned out to be a space-age scooter that could balance itself as it carried people down sidewalks. NASCAR driver Dale Earnhardt died in a crash on the last lap of the Daytona 500.

In 2001, the Israeli-Palestinian conflict grew worse, as Palestinian terrorists conducted suicide bombings in Israel. Voters in the Jewish state elected Ariel Sharon as their prime minister—a fierce critic of the process to create a Palestinian state in the Occupied Territories in return for peace between Palestinians and Israelis. A group of 178 nations came to an agreement, without the United States, to limit greenhouse gas emissions—human-produced carbon dioxide believed to be responsible for climate change. U.S.-China tensions grew as a Chinese fighter jet collided in midair with an American spy plane, which made an emergency landing in China.

In 2001, al Qaeda terrorists inflicted the worst attack in history on American soil, killing almost three thousand people. Following the attack, the economy, which had already been slowing down, came to a halt and 415,000 people lost their jobs that October. The U.S. invaded Afghanistan to pursue al Qaeda's leaders and their Taliban hosts.

## 43

During the weeks leading up to George W. Bush's inauguration as the forty-third president, the media debated how the new leader could reunite the country and heal the wounds from the election. There was talk of him adopting a more moderate agenda, or appointing several Democrats to his cabinet. But Bush stressed that while he would try to cooperate with Democrats, he had won the election and would work to enact the agenda he had campaigned on.

His proposed cabinet included only one Democrat. But if it lacked much bipartisanship, it did have plenty of experience, especially in national security. Colin Powell, a moderate Republican who had served as National Security Advisor under Ronald Reagan and chairman of the Joint Chiefs of Staff during the Gulf War under Bush's father, would be secretary of state. National Security Advisor Condoleezza Rice was a veteran of George H. W. Bush's White House, too. Donald Rumsfeld, the new secretary of defense, had held that job once before, under President Gerald Ford.

And then there was the vice president. Since the president was new to Washington, while Cheney had spent much of his adult life in Congress, the White House, or the Pentagon, Bush valued his guidance greatly, giving him several key assignments and always asking his advice.

On Saturday, January 20, Bush and President Clinton drove together to the Capitol for the inauguration. The crowd was smaller than expected, mainly because of temperatures in the thirties and a cold rain. The wounds from the recount battle were not over—protesters carried signs reading "Hail to the Thief." Bush took the oath of office and spoke to the crowd for fifteen minutes. He called for a new sense of unity and challenged Americans to help their neighbors.

Then he got to work implementing his agenda. The main message stressed by the White House staff during the first few months was: This is a professional administration. Clinton had come to Washington eight years earlier with a lot of bold ideas but a staff largely new to federal government, and had struggled in his first two years. Bush appointed a team with experience. Several staffers told reporters they wanted to make it clear to the country that the grown-ups were back in charge.

That attitude, coupled with the staff's impressive discipline and constant repeating of the same message over and over, helped Bush enact his two top domestic policy priorities during his first six months. First came his proposed tax cut package, which would cost the government $1.3 trillion over nine years. Bush had an easy time convincing Congress to pass the tax cut, persuading several Democrats in both the House and Senate to vote for it. Bush was also able to build bipartisan support for his education reforms, the No Child Left Behind Act, which linked federal education funds to public school students' performance on standardized tests.

But after those two legislative successes, Bush's domestic agenda bogged down. Several of his environmental policies drew widespread criticism—his staff discounted the growing evidence of climate change and pushed hard to open public lands to more coal mining and oil and gas drilling. He opposed a popular bill to protect people from questionable practices by health insurance companies.

On foreign policy, many members of the Bush team, including Cheney and Rumsfeld, believed the Clinton administration had been too willing to cooperate with international bodies like the United Nations and to intervene in conflicts that had no direct impact on the U.S. They believed that American foreign policy had to stress American interests and that, as the lone superpower, America had the ability to implement its objectives without international groups like the U.N.

In its first six months, the administration withdrew support for a planned International Criminal Court that would try war criminals. The Bush team said it would not support a court that might try to prosecute U.S. soldiers or citizens. Bush also ended U.S. participation in the Kyoto Protocols, an international agreement to curtail greenhouse gas emissions, because the administration believed imposing rules on emissions might hurt American businesses.

## THE PROLIFERATION PROBLEM

A top foreign policy priority for the Bush team was a ballistic missile defense system.

When Bush took office, the Cold War had been over for ten years, and the biggest threat to U.S. security was no longer the Soviet Union's large nuclear arsenal, but small, rogue countries that might try to develop or buy a few nuclear missiles. Nuclear proliferation, the spread of nuclear weapon technology, had been a concern since the Soviet Union's collapse. The lead-

## THE HIDDEN KINGDOM

North Korea is one of the most isolated nations on earth. It's governed by a communist regime that keeps its people cut off from the outside world in order to maintain power, even though this has caused extreme poverty. The U.S. government has struggled for decades to figure out how to deal with North Korea.

The Korean peninsula was once one nation, but after forty years of occupation and war, it was divided into two separate countries in 1948: a communist dictatorship in the northern half, the Democratic People's Republic of Korea; and a democracy in the south, the Republic of Korea.

In 1950, North Korean leader Kim Il-Sung invaded South Korea. After four years of war, which involved both Koreas, the United States, the United Nations, and China, the fighting ended but no treaty was ever signed. The border remains one of the world's most militarized spots, with North Korean forces on one side and U.S. and South Korean forces on the other.

Today, South Korea is the world's twelfth most prosperous nation, while North Korea is impoverished. The North Korean people have no idea of what goes on outside their borders. A massive network of spies reports anyone who speaks out against the regime. When someone does, they and their family members are taken away to a prison camp.

ing suspect on the list of rogue nations was North Korea, which already had nuclear fuel that could be turned into a weapon.

North Korean president Kim Il-Sung had dreamed of developing a nuclear weapon since the Korean War, when his nation had lived in fear of an American nuclear strike. By the eighties, he had a nuclear reactor powered by uranium. That uranium could be reprocessed into another element, plutonium, an ideal fuel for nuclear weapons.

In 1994, President Clinton made an agreement with Kim's son Kim Jong-Il,

*Kim Jong-Il meets with Korean army personnel, 1988. Bush wanted the North Koreans to give up fuel that could potentially be used for nuclear weapons.*

who had become North Korea's leader—operations were frozen at the reactor and inspectors from the International Atomic Energy Agency (IAEA) would stay there and make sure the spent fuel remained untouched. In return, the U.S. would help North Korea meet its energy needs.

Within a few months of taking office, Bush and his team broke off talks with North Korea. Several of Bush's advisers, including Cheney and Rumsfeld, condemned the 1994 agreement because it did not set a firm deadline for North Korea to give up the nuclear fuel. Worse, they believed the energy assistance to the North helped Kim keep his government in power. The Bush administration hoped that sanctions and diplomatic pressure could trigger a collapse of Kim's authority.

## AL QAEDA'S SECOND STRIKE

One of Bush's other early foreign policy dilemmas surfaced just five days after he was inaugurated. On January 25, the CIA briefed the new president on a terrorist attack that took place while he was still a candidate. On October 12, 2000, an American naval destroyer, the U.S.S. *Cole*, had docked in the port of Aden in the Middle Eastern country of Yemen. Two men pulled up alongside in a small boat, waving to the crew. Before the sailors could respond, the boat exploded. The blast ripped a forty-by-sixty-foot gash in the side of the *Cole*, hitting the ship's galley. Seventeen sailors were killed. The survivors rushed to control the flooding and keep the ship afloat.

CIA and FBI investigators came to believe the attack was the work of al Qaeda, a terrorist group founded by a wealthy Saudi Arabian named Osama bin Laden, who was known to have attacked Americans overseas at least once before. Who exactly was this terrorist leader?

Bin Laden was the son of one of Saudi Arabia's wealthiest men—the late Mohammed bin Laden, a Yemeni who emigrated to Saudi Arabia and built a construction business empire. Mohammed was a favorite of the Saudi royal family, and he had many children, some of whom had lived in the United States and Europe and were quite cosmopolitan. Osama was one of his younger sons. He had a degree in engineering, but turned his focus to Islamist politics while in college.

Osama bin Laden speaks to reporters from an undisclosed location in Afghanistan, date unknown.

In the mid-eighties, bin Laden traveled to Pakistan and worked with one of his old professors to establish an organization aiding Muslim fighters in the Afghan-Soviet War.

# THE RUSSIAN BEAR VS. THE HOLY WARRIORS

In 1979, the Soviet Union invaded a small nation to its south—Afghanistan. Their goal was to prop up the communist government there. But the Afghan people resisted Soviet control. And the U.S., eager to keep the Soviets from moving closer to the oil-rich Persian Gulf, backed the rebellious Afghans.

Afghans fighting the Soviets called themselves mujahedin, Arabic for holy warriors. The CIA, Pakistani intelligence, and Saudi Arabia's government all began supporting these mujahedin. The Saudis, who wanted to support their fellow Sunni Muslims, joined with the U.S. to provide money and weapons. (Sunni Islam is the largest branch of Islam, the form of the Muslim faith followed by about 85 percent of the world's 1.5 billion Muslims. Because Islam began in what is now Saudi Arabia, the Saudis consider themselves special protectors of Sunni Islam.) The Pakistanis, who did not want the Soviets as next-door neighbors, channeled the aid to various mujahedin groups.

While the intelligence agencies provided a great deal of the aid, the other large portion came from Sunnis around the world. This aid was built on two Islamic principles—zakat and jihad. Zakat is charity—one of the major beliefs of Islam is that all Muslims should give some of their wealth to those in need. Helping Muslims in Afghanistan fight the Soviets was considered a worthy cause. Jihad is a more complicated principle. It means struggle—Islam teaches that man must struggle for his faith. Some Muslims interpret jihad as the personal struggle to be a good Muslim. For a few Muslims, jihad means physically fighting against nonbelievers. To them, combat against non-Muslims such as the Soviets was a holy war.

An entire mujahedin industry sprang up. Money flowed from both the intelligence agencies and various Sunni Muslim charities. Volunteers hoping to wage jihad arrived from all over the Muslim world to help the Afghans fight. The mujahedin also recruited young men from madrassas, religious schools, in Pakistan and sent them to training camps along the Afghan-Pakistan border.

For ten years, the mujahedin resisted the Soviets, never defeating them, but constantly harassing them. The Soviets pulled out in 1989, frustrated at all the money and men they were losing while failing to subdue the Afghan rebels. After the Soviets left, America withdrew its aid to the Afghan fighters and to Pakistan. The U.S. government believed that with the Soviets gone, America had no interest in Afghanistan.

Afghan mujahedin leaders attempted to form a new government, but they ended up fighting each other. While there was an official Afghan government in the capital of Kabul, some cabinet ministers were trying to topple it, even shelling the city with artillery. This fighting continued for nine years. Other mujahedin leaders simply carved out little fiefdoms in parts of the country for themselves, forcing the people to pay taxes to them, profiting from Afghanistan's poppy crop, which was sold overseas to make heroin.

Many of the foreign fighters returned to their home countries, committed to using their skills and Islamist ideas to overthrow their own governments. Some stayed in Afghanistan, using it as a base to train more holy warriors. Afghan training camps that had prepared men to fight the Soviets began training them to launch terrorist attacks.

After the war, Osama bin Laden created an organization to spread Islamist jihad to other countries. Bin Laden hopes to change the Muslim world because he is an extreme Islamist. Islamism is sometimes known as political Islam. It is a set of political and religious beliefs inspired by some of the earliest traditions of Islam and the prophet Muhammad. When Muhammad began preaching in the seventh century, establishing Islam, he and his advisers set out laws for Muslim society, called sharia. Some Muslims believe sharia is simply a personal code of behavior. Islamists believe majority Muslim countries should use sharia as a basis for their laws. Extreme Islamists, including bin Laden, believe that all Muslims should be ruled by a strict interpretation of sharia.

Most of the nations of the Middle East are ruled by dictators or monarchs who are Muslim but do not rule by strict Muslim ideas. Bin Laden wanted to create a new Muslim society ruled by strict sharia. He found some sympathy for his ideas, especially in the Middle East, where many Muslims wished their leaders were less corrupt. But the Islamist extremists' version of Islam was too intolerant for most Muslims.

Bin Laden dubbed his new oragnization al Qaeda, which means "the base." And he began to vocally blame America for the Muslim world's problems. He denounced the Saudi royal family for allowing American troops to live on military bases in Saudi Arabia, home to Islam's holiest sites, the cities of Mecca and Medina. In 1992, the ruling family exiled him.

Forced from his homeland, bin Laden moved to Sudan, where he began building al Qaeda into a global terrorist organization. Al Qaeda was part of a new breed of terrorist groups. It was a loose network, with alliances and connections to organizations around the world with similar extreme ideas. Globalization, with its flow of ideas, allowed these terrorists to link up and share tactics, money, and contacts.

Bin Laden's main target was now America. Why? Many Islamists were hostile toward America. Partially this hostility was because of American support for corrupt leaders in the Middle East. Partially it was because of American support for Israel, which most Islamists believed was built on land that should belong to Palestinians. But it was also because America was the world's most powerful nation. Its culture and ideals were spreading across the globe, in movies, music, and on the Internet. Some radical Islamists hated America simply because it was America.

Bin Laden believed that attacking America was symbolic. He hoped to inspire Muslims worldwide to unite and drive Americans out of their countries and overthrow insufficiently pious leaders.

The CIA knew about bin Laden but did not completely understand his role in terrorism. But by 2000, they had seen enough to know he was dangerous.

## STUDENTS OF ISLAM

In 1996, accompanied by his top deputies—including leading Egyptian Islamist Ayman al Zawahiri—bin Laden decided to go back to where he had started al Qaeda: Afghanistan. The country had endured almost twenty years of war. Almost three million Afghans had fled into Pakistan's border region during the fighting, living in miserable camps. Their sons attended madrassas, most of which were sponsored by conservative Islamic charities or Islamist groups. Their daughters were not allowed to attend madrassas, and there were very few other schools, so most girls received no education. Madrassas taught a very strict interpretation of Islam—they were incubators for future extreme Islamists.

In 1994, two years before bin Laden's arrival, a new band of fighters had appeared in the southern part of the country, attacking local warlords and taking control of towns. They called themselves the Taliban, which means "students of Islam." Most were former mujahedin and also Pashtuns, the largest ethnic group in Afghanistan. In October, they took over Kandahar, the largest city in the south and the traditional capital of Pashtun territory.

The Taliban soon gained an important ally—the Pakistani government. Pakistan was very much interested in who controlled Afghanistan. Much of Pakistan's foreign policy was rooted in its deep hostility toward India, its eastern neighbor. The government wanted to make sure India did not gain a foothold in the west by establishing friendly relations with Afghanistan.

Leaders of Pakistan's spy agency, the Inter-Services Intelligence (ISI), decided that Pakistan should support the Taliban, and they convinced Prime Minister Benazir Bhutto to aid them. ISI fed guns and money to the group. It encouraged young Pakistani Islamists and Afghan refugees to cross into Afghanistan and fight for the Taliban.

Thanks to this aid, the Taliban gained control of most of Afghanistan by 1998. While Afghanistan had always been a conservative country, with most Muslim women covering their hair and many wearing a burqa—a full-length gown that hid the face and body from strangers—the Islamist Taliban now instituted an extreme version of sharia. All women were ordered to wear the burqa, and were barred from school, work, or sports. Half the population effectively vanished from sight. Men were ordered to stop trimming their beards. Music, videos, TV, movies, alcohol, paintings of people, photographic portraits, playing cards, dolls, stuffed animals, and kite flying were all banned. A squad of religious policemen roamed the streets, beating with sticks anyone deemed to be violating these rules. Thieves had their hands amputated.

When bin Laden arrived in 1996, he stayed near Jalalabad, on the border with

Pakistan, with an old local ally from the Soviet War. But after the Taliban took control of Kabul, he met with their leader, Mullah Mohammed Omar, who invited him to stay near Kandahar. So bin Laden moved his entire operation to Kandahar province. He set up training camps for aspiring terrorists. In return for Omar's hospitality, bin Laden provided the Taliban with money and fighters to help in their campaign to defeat the last remaining non-Taliban mujahedin forces and completely conquer Afghanistan. Al Qaeda and the Taliban were separate groups, but they were now closely allied.

The training camps were an ideal operation for bin Laden. Al Qaeda leaders could pass on their knowledge to aspiring jihadis, who were then sent to various Islamist terrorist groups in other countries. Secure in Afghanistan, bin Laden began making bigger plans for al Qaeda.

As early as 1993, the CIA listed bin Laden as a terrorist financier. In 1996, as the agency began to see terrorism as a bigger threat and put more resources into counterterrorism, it created a special unit at headquarters focused on bin Laden. But it had little idea of his ambitious objectives.

In 1996, a member of al Qaeda walked into a U.S. embassy in Africa and offered to provide intelligence on the organization in return for sanctuary. He explained that al Qaeda had a "military committee" planning attacks on the United States. The group was trying to obtain "weapons of mass destruction"—chemical or biological weapons or nuclear material. A federal grand jury indicted bin Laden in 1996 on terrorism charges. He was now a wanted man.

By late 1997, the CIA had developed a plan to send local Afghans to capture bin Laden. But they believed it had only a 40 percent chance of working. The State Department also asked the Taliban government to expel bin Laden from Afghanistan. But it refused, insisting he was no threat to America and it was against Islamic custom to expel a guest.

In February of 1998, bin Laden issued what he called a fatwa, which traditionally is a religious declaration by a Muslim cleric, claiming that America had declared war on Allah and his people, and that every Muslim had a duty to kill Americans wherever and whenever possible. In a TV interview that summer, he said, "We do not differentiate between those dressed in military uniforms and civilians; they are all targets."

On the morning of August 7, 1998, two

# LEARNING COUNTERTERRORISM

While few Americans knew much about bin Laden, there were people in the U.S. government actively trying to stop him and al Qaeda. But throughout the nineties, U.S. intelligence agencies were hampered by two problems: counterterrorism is handled by several agencies, and none of these had been designed to fight a modern terrorist group like al Qaeda.

**The Federal Bureau of Investigation** traditionally investigated attacks against American citizens, both in the U.S. and abroad. But the FBI is a law enforcement organization—it looks for evidence that can be used in a court of law to convict terrorists. (Terrorists see themselves as soldiers or political activists. Throughout the eighties and nineties, the U.S. government viewed them as criminals and believed that treating a terrorist like an ordinary murderer took away his claim of fighting for a legitimate political cause.) Much of the FBI's evidence, because of legal rules, cannot be shared with others. That makes it hard for agents to exchange information with people in other agencies. Also, the Bureau mostly focuses on more common crimes, such as drug trafficking and financial fraud.

**The Central Intelligence Agency** is America's top foreign intelligence organization, gathering information overseas and conducting covert operations. But it was designed at the start of the Cold War to spy on the Soviets and their allies. Few CIA agents knew Arabic or the languages of Southern Asia and even fewer were trying to infiltrate al Qaeda.

**The National Security Agency** is responsible for monitoring all sorts of electronic communications like phone calls or email, looking for messages from suspected enemies of the U.S. But by the late nineties, there was so much electronic communication that the NSA was struggling to analyze it all.

All three of these agencies and other members of the "Intelligence Community" were supposed to share information. In reality, they shared little, sometimes because members were unsure of which classified information they were allowed to share. Several times in the nineties, different agencies held different pieces of information that, if they had been connected, might have helped fight terrorism.

trucks carrying bombs drove into U.S. embassies in two East African countries—Kenya and Tanzania. The bombs exploded, killing 12 Americans and 201 others in Kenya and 11 people in Tanzania. The CIA and FBI found evidence the attacks were the work of al Qaeda. Thirteen days later, President Clinton ordered U.S. ships to fire cruise missiles at targets including a terrorist camp near Kandahar, but bin Laden had left the camp a few hours earlier.

When President Bush was briefed on al Qaeda's role in the *Cole* bombing, he quickly felt trapped in the same debate Clinton had faced in his final two years in office. He did not want to launch more cruise missiles, which he felt were ineffective. But there was no support in America for taking stronger military action in Afghanistan. So Bush asked his team to devise a new comprehensive strategy not just for fighting al Qaeda but for dealing with the whole region.

Some, especially Richard Clarke, the National Security Council's counterterrorism chief, argued that such a review would take too long. But terrorism was not a top issue on Bush's agenda. The stream of intelligence during the summer of 2001 warning of possible plots (including a briefing memo given to the president titled "Bin Laden determined to attack U.S.") did not trigger fast action. The principal members of the National Security Council did not meet to discuss al Qaeda until September 4, eight months after Bush took office.

## THE PLANES OPERATION

Because of the shortcomings of the intelligence system and creative planning by al Qaeda, Bush's staff did not know that members of al Qaeda were already living in the United States, part of a five-year plot to attack America at home.

In 1996, Khalid Sheikh Mohammed, an Islamist terrorist whose nephew had set off a powerful bomb in the World Trade Center parking garage in New York City in 1993, met with bin Laden in Afghanistan. He told bin Laden about an idea he had—a plan to attack the American homeland. In 1998, bin Laden approved the idea. They discussed potential targets in Washington, D.C., and New York, and bin Laden began recruiting members of al Qaeda to undertake the mission. Two Saudi al Qaeda members arrived in Los Angeles in January of 2000. At the same time, four young Middle Eastern men—students who had met and lived together in Hamburg, Germany—

arrived at an al Qaeda training camp in Afghanistan. Bin Laden quickly realized they were ideal for his plot.

Mohamed Atta, from Egypt, who was bin Laden's pick to lead the operation, Marwan al Shehhi, from the United Arab Emirates, Ziad Jarrah, from Lebanon, and Ramzi Bin al Shibh, from Yemen, had not been known as Islamists at home, but in Hamburg, where Muslims were a minority, they began associating with radical Islamists, several of whom preached the virtue of jihad. They became more pious, conservative, and outspoken against America and Israel. Finally, they traveled to Afghanistan.

It's unknown why bin Laden picked four newcomers for his plan. One possibility is that because they had lived in a Western country they would be able to blend in living in America. They also had no past history of terrorist activities and would not arouse suspicion.

In the early summer of 2000, all of the men except Bin al Shibh, who had been denied a visa, arrived separately in the U.S. They enrolled in flight schools in Florida, training to fly planes and living otherwise quiet lives. Later that summer, another al Qaeda recruit, a Saudi named Hani Hanjour who had learned to fly in Arizona in the nineties, arrived in the U.S. and began refresher courses at flight schools.

In May of 2001, Atta began greeting several new arrivals. Al Qaeda sent fifteen recruits to join up with the four pilots-in-training. They were in their twenties, with little education, and had been recruited by various Islamist clerics who ran mosques and other organizations in Saudi Arabia. (More moderate clerics called one of these mosques a "terrorist factory.") The young men ended up in Pakistan, and then terrorist training camps in Afghanistan. They filled out a questionnaire that asked about their backgrounds, skills, and whether they would be willing to participate in "martyrdom" operations—suicide attacks. Bin Laden met and personally selected the operatives for the mission in the U.S. They were given special training but few details. All they knew was that they were on a suicide mission.

During the summer of 2001, all the al Qaeda members found apartments in the U.S., mostly in Florida. They got driver's licenses, joined gyms, and generally blended in. The four pilot trainees took a series of cross-country trips, flying from cities like New York to San Francisco. And then, in late August, Atta bought plane tickets for four more flights.

# 2001

## *September to December*

### WE HAVE SOME PLANES . . .

TUESDAY, SEPTEMBER 11, 2001, was a gorgeous day in New York City. Warm, sunny, without a cloud in the sky. At 8:46 A.M., many people on the streets looked up and saw a Boeing 767 flying lower than usual over Manhattan. Then the plane plowed into the top floors of the World Trade Center's North Tower. A fireball exploded from the building's ninety-third through ninety-ninth floors.

Earlier that morning, the al Qaeda members boarded four flights. Atta and al Shehhi, each with four partners, boarded separate flights from Boston to Los Angeles. Jarrah, with three partners, boarded a United Airlines flight in Newark heading to San Francisco. Hani Hanjour and four partners boarded an American Airlines flight in Washington heading to Los Angeles.

Tuesday is a quiet travel day—all of the planes had fewer passengers than on other days. But each plane was fully loaded with fuel for the long trip cross-country. The men were armed with small knives and mace. The knives were not illegal under air travel security rules at that time, and the men had not been heavily searched at airport checkpoints.

Shortly after American Airlines flight 11 took off, two of the al Qaeda members stabbed some of the flight attendants and

*The second hijacked plane strikes the South Tower of the World Trade Center, not long after the North Tower was hit, on September 11, 2001.*

entered the cockpit. Atta took over at the controls. According to two attendants who called the airline, the men had also stabbed a passenger, sprayed mace in the air, and chased everyone toward the back of the jet. The plane was rapidly descending and changing course. One of the hijackers, trying to speak to the cabin, accidentally keyed the radio to air traffic controllers. "We have some planes," he said. "Nobody move. Everything will be OK. Just stay quiet."

Similar scenes unfolded on the other planes. With cold precision, the hijackers fought their way into the cockpits, took control of the planes, and rerouted them.

It was Atta's plane that slammed into the North Tower at 8:46 A.M. All ninety-two people on board were killed instantly. So were many people on the floors the plane hit. Black smoke began to billow out of the windows, and jet fuel, office furniture, and plane parts began falling to the ground far below.

At first, it all looked like a horrible accident. Fire engines and ambulances began rushing in from all parts of the city. The emergency responders set up a base camp in the lobby of the building and headed up the stairs to get to people in the tower. They realized very quickly that they did not have enough resources to put out the fire anytime soon. Their mission was to evacuate the building.

The plane had damaged all the emergency stairwells; everyone from the ninety-second to the one hundred tenth floors was trapped. People on the floors below struggled to descend the stairs. There was plenty of confusion. Intercoms didn't work. Firefighter radios worked poorly inside the stairwells. Calls to 911 overloaded the emergency phone system. Next door, in the South Tower, conflicting announcements were made about whether occupants should stay or evacuate.

With Marwan al Shehhi at the controls, United Airlines flight 175 had flown south of New York, circled, and headed back toward Manhattan. The plane sliced into the South Tower, between the seventy-seventh and eighty-fifth floors, at 9:03. Many people watching now realized this was no accident. It was an attack. And it wasn't over. At 9:41, witnesses on a highway across the river from Washington, D.C., watched a 757 fly low over the road and slam into the side of the Pentagon. Everyone on board and 125 people inside the building were killed. Part of the building collapsed and emergency crews rushed to evacuate the wounded.

Meanwhile, air traffic controllers were desperately trying to find the fourth hijacked plane. But the passengers of flight

93 had learned by cell phone what had happened in New York and Northern Virginia. They decided to try and take the plane back. They rushed the hijackers, fighting to get into the cockpit. Jarrah, at the controls, realized they would reach him. He plunged the plane straight down, and it crashed into a Pennsylvania field, killing all on board. The plane had been heading for D.C. to strike either the U.S. Capitol or the White House.

Back in New York, people were trying desperately to get out of the World Trade Center. As firefighters, police officers, and other emergency responders rushed up the stairs, office workers tried to get down. People called loved ones from stairwells, unsure if they would survive.

Just before 9:59, witnesses on the nearby streets heard a rumble. The South Tower teetered and then collapsed in a matter of seconds, killing everyone inside, as well as many people in the plaza below and in surrounding buildings. The jet fuel from the plane had sparked a fire in the tower that reached 2,000 degrees Fahrenheit. The steel and concrete on the burning floors melted and could no longer support the weight of the floors above. As the top floors came crashing down, the entire building imploded. A huge cloud of dust and ash crashed like a wave on the surrounding streets. Most of downtown Manhattan was obscured for a few minutes.

When people could see again, the emergency teams began issuing a frantic order for everyone to evacuate the North Tower. Many firefighters began heading down, helping whomever they could. Others did not hear the order. At 10:28, the tower collapsed, killing almost everyone inside. Al Qaeda's attack was complete—in all, an estimated 2,973 people were dead.

## RESPONSE

President Bush was getting ready to read to schoolchildren in Florida when the attacks began. He was arriving at an elementary school when an adviser told him a plane had hit the World Trade Center. It was assumed to be an accident. Bush was reading to the students when the second plane hit. His chief of staff whispered the news in Bush's ear. The president tried to look calm and in charge, and waited a few minutes before leaving. He spoke to his staff and headed to the airport for Air Force One.

At 9:30, Vice President Cheney was in his White House office, trying to learn what was happening in New York, when Secret Service agents came in the room and ordered him out. With the third plane in Washington airspace, they worried the White House was a target and rushed him to a bunker underneath the building. There he called the president. During their conversation, Bush said, "Somebody's going to pay."

The Secret Service did not want Bush to return to Washington yet, despite the president's objections. No one seemed to know if more planes had been hijacked or if other attacks were planned. Bush spent the day flying to various military bases. He spoke with his top advisers by video teleconference. CIA Director George Tenet said early signs pointed to al Qaeda as the perpetrator. All nonemergency civilian aircraft were grounded for the first time in history. The military was at a heightened state of readiness.

When Bush arrived in Washington that night, he addressed the nation, saying, "We will make no distinction between the terrorists who committed these acts and those who harbor them." He then met with his top advisers to discuss military options.

The nation was in shock. Most Americans struggled to understand why anyone would do something like this. In New York, rescue crews were too busy to pause. They were digging through the World Trade Center, now a pile of rubble several square blocks across, hoping to find survivors.

Around the world, people offered support. France's leading newspaper's front page declared, "*Nous sommes tous Américains*," meaning "We Are All Americans." Israel and Ireland held national days of mourning. Even Iran and Cuba, longtime enemies of the U.S., issued statements condemning the attack. In Iran's capital, Tehran, a moment of silence was held before a soccer match.

The next day, shock was replaced by fear. What if there were more terrorists in the U.S.? What if more attacks were planned? Planes remained grounded until new security measures could be implemented. Security was heightened at borders and ports. And the FBI was looking for suspects—other al Qaeda operatives or people who may have helped the hijackers.

Working with immigration authorities and police, FBI agents arrested 768 foreigners, mostly Middle Eastern men and other Muslims, for various immigration violations, and held them while looking into any possible terrorism connections. Normally, many of the arrested would have been eligible for bail, but all bail was denied. The immigrants were held for an average of eighty days. In the end, only eight were detained for further investigation. Most of the others were deported for unrelated immigration violations.

Just a week after the attacks, the Bush administration sent an ultimatum to the Taliban—turn over al Qaeda's leadership and close down the terrorist training camps, or we will destroy al Qaeda and the camps. On September 20, Bush addressed Congress and the nation. "The enemy of America is not our many Muslim friends. Our enemy is a radical network of terrorists and every government that supports them. Every nation now has a decision to make: Either you are with us, or you are with the terrorists." Bush also said the "global war on terror" he was launching did not end with al Qaeda. "It will not end until every terror group of global reach has been found, stopped, and defeated."

But Americans' fear only grew as they learned how easily the hijackers had been able to live inside the country and execute their attacks. America prided itself on being an open society. Now politicians, the media, and citizens realized how many targets there were. What if al Qaeda attacked nuclear power plants or water reservoirs or public transit? What if the terrorists used biological, chemical, or nuclear weapons next?

On October 5, a photo editor at a tabloid newspaper in Florida died from anthrax, a disease caused by deadly bacteria. Someone had mailed five letters filled with anthrax spores to media outlets. Two more letters were mailed to Democratic senators. In all, five people died from the spores and seventeen others were infected.

Several administration officials and members of the media speculated that the anthrax may have come from an alliance between al Qaeda and Iraq. In 1991, the U.S. and an international coalition had fought a war with Iraq, which was ruled by a dictator named Saddam Hussein who had developed chemical and biological weapons before the conflict. Ever since the end of that war, the U.S. and the United Nations had been using sanctions to try and force Saddam to prove that he had ended his weapons of mass destruction (WMD) programs and destroyed his WMD stockpiles. He refused to fully comply. That made Saddam a natural suspect in the anthrax attacks, in the eyes of many members of the Bush administration. But seven months after the attacks, analysis of the spores showed they had originated in a U.S. military lab. The FBI began investigating American scientists instead.

In the frightened atmosphere after 9/11 and the anthrax attacks, the president asked Congress for stronger law enforcement powers to fight terrorism inside the country. On October 26, 2001, Bush signed the USA PATRIOT Act. It increased agencies' powers to search telephone records and emails, eased restrictions on intelligence gathering inside the country, and enhanced the discretion of the authorities in detaining and deporting immigrants suspected of terrorism-related acts. The act was supported by both parties and passed by wide margins in both houses of Congress.

But some critics questioned whether the law went too far. America had been founded on the principle of individual liberty. Now, the government was being allowed to snoop into people's phone conversations and their emails, even to find out what books they checked out from libraries. Could the government be trusted to investigate only terrorism suspects, or would it use these powers to harass political opponents? Was America giving up its freedom for security?

## FIGHTING BACK

The Bush team moved quickly to go after al Qaeda's leadership in Afghanistan. Lack of political will to send forces there was no longer a problem. The Pentagon began developing plans. Colin Powell and the State Department began gathering a coalition of allied nations. America's European allies, especially Great Britain and other members of NATO, promised a great deal of military support. Several Central Asian nations to the north of Afghanistan offered the U.S. use of their military bases. But the most important potential ally was Pakistan.

To successfully invade Afghanistan, depose the Taliban, and capture al Qaeda's leaders, the U.S. needed Pakistani support. In the days after 9/11, the State Department presented Pakistan's ambassador with a list of demands, calling on its government to denounce the attacks, cut off support for the Taliban, and allow the U.S. to use Pakistan as a base for its move into Afghanistan.

Pakistani leader Pervez Musharraf, a general who had taken power in a coup two years earlier, knew he could not say no. Bush's statements made it clear that the U.S. would take strong action against any nation providing aid to terrorists. Administration officials were quietly telling the press that they were looking for evidence that other countries had helped al Qaeda—particularly countries with a history of supporting terrorists, like Iraq, Libya, Sudan, or Iran. If Pakistan refused, Bush might decide its support for the Taliban was evidence enough that the U.S. should invade Pakistan too, or he might impose painful economic sanctions. Musharraf agreed to Bush's demands. But he told his leading deputies that Pakistan would

# PARTITION NATION

No nation played a bigger role in Afghanistan's affairs before 9/11 than Pakistan. For decades, Pakistan had been trying to influence who governed its neighbor. Understanding Pakistan's goals in Afghanistan requires knowing its history.

Pakistan was created when Great Britain ended its control of Imperial India in 1947. A majority of Indians were Hindu, while many others were Muslims and Sikhs. When a Muslim political party expressed worry that Muslims would be second-class citizens in an independent India and called for a separate Islamic nation, the British complied by dividing the territory into two countries—Pakistan and India. Areas where the population was more than 50 percent Muslim became Pakistan, and areas where more than 50 percent were Hindu became India.

After the borders were demarcated, many of the Hindus and Sikhs in Pakistan migrated to India, while Muslims in India migrated to Pakistan. An estimated 25 million people uprooted their lives and moved to new lands. Religious tensions flared and violence broke out—anywhere from 500,000 to 1 million people died. Meanwhile, both Pakistan and India claimed the territory of Kashmir, and both sent troops to the area. After a war, India controlled 60 percent of Kashmir, while Pakistan controlled the rest.

Pakistan's hostility toward India has only grown since. The two countries have fought two more wars and several minor conflicts. By the early seventies, both were in a desperate race to develop nuclear weapons. India tested a nuclear device in 1974, Pakistan in 1998. The military became the strongest institution in Pakistan—several times, generals overthrew democratically elected leaders.

Beginning in the seventies, Pakistani leaders began embracing Islamism. The government helped madrassas and Islamic charities. The spy agency, the ISI, provided support to Islamist militants, who attacked Indian soldiers in Kashmir. When the Pakistanis helped channel American aid to the Afghan mujahedin, they favored the Islamist fighters. And in the nineties the government backed the Taliban in Afghanistan. The Pakistanis were afraid that India would one day gain influence with an Afghan government, sandwiching Pakistan between two hostile nations. They believed that having an Islamist group like the Taliban in power in Afghanistan would keep India out.

Pakistan and America had been allies since the Cold War—both opposed the Soviet Union. But after the Soviets left Afghanistan, America cut back aid to Pakistan and largely ignored it for a decade. Most Pakistanis believed America was unreliable at best, and some thought it was anti-Islamic.

only support the U.S. for now, and would look after its own interests when it came to the long-term future of Afghanistan. He believed the Americans would not stay in the region forever. They would leave, just as they had after the Soviets withdrew in 1989.

At the Pentagon, Rumsfeld and the generals struggled to plan the invasion of Afghanistan. The Taliban fought on foot or in Toyota pickup trucks—not much of a target for America's sophisticated airpower. Rumsfeld was very worried about invading with a large force and then getting bogged down as the Soviets had.

While some ground troops were sent to the region in case they proved necessary, Rumsfeld's plan centered on smaller groups of special operations forces and CIA agents. Teams of CIA agents began sneaking into Afghanistan in late September. Carrying suitcases full of money, they met with various factions of the Northern Alliance—a group of mujahedin still resisting Taliban rule—and struck up a partnership. With American cash and support, the Alliance launched an offensive against the Taliban. They got more support when U.S. Special Forces soldiers arrived. One crucial job of the Special Forces was to pinpoint Taliban targets so U.S. planes could drop bombs, inflicting heavy damage.

The results were rapid. With American help, the Northern Alliance was able to push the Taliban out of major cities in the north within a month. The Taliban abandoned Kabul on November 12. By December, the Taliban had fled Kandahar, its last stronghold.

But there was a price to Rumsfeld's streamlined war. As of December, there were only 1,300 American troops on the ground in Afghanistan. It was one thing to drive the Taliban out of power; it was another to control the country. The U.S. relied on the Northern Alliance and other warlords to capture al Qaeda members. Many fleeing terrorists were able to simply bribe their would-be captors and escape into Pakistan.

Bin Laden himself retreated to a mountain called Tora Bora on the Afghan-Pakistan border, which had an extensive network of caves. The Americans sent three warlords and their men in to try and capture or kill bin Laden and his supporters. U.S. Special Forces soldiers arrived three days after the battle started. American bombers pounded the mountains, but while the fighting raged, al Qaeda's leaders simply sneaked across the border into Pakistan's tribal areas. Pakistan did nothing to stop them.

Pakistan's tribal areas were a perfect place for al Qaeda members to hide. The

*An American special operations soldier guards a helicopter in Kwaja Bahauddin, Afghanistan, November 15, 2001.*

people were Pashtuns, like the Taliban, and were more loyal to their tribes than to Pakistan's central government. Soon, al Qaeda began sending out videotaped messages from bin Laden, proving he had survived.

## A NEW HOPE . . . AND A NEW WAR

For the Afghan people, there was new hope with the fall of the Taliban. International leaders and Afghans met and selected an interim government for the country. Northern Alliance members claimed many of the top posts, but Hamid Karzai, a Pashtun tribal leader from Helmand, near Kandahar, secured the presidency. Karzai began trying to gain control over a shattered country.

Back in the U.S. there was jubilation at the success in Afghanistan, even though al Qaeda's top leaders were still at large. Bush's popularity soared. Plenty of fear remained, but the first wave in Bush's war on terror appeared successful. And it was about to be expanded. In November, Bush took Rumsfeld aside after a meeting. He wanted to know what kind of plans the Pentagon had for invading Iraq. He wasn't sure they would be necessary, but he wanted the military to be ready.

# 2002

## *An Axis of Evil*

IN 2002, A young woman from Texas named Kelly Clarkson won a competition to become a pop star on a new series called *American Idol.* Bruce Springsteen's latest album, *The Rising*, focused on widows, soldiers, and emergency personnel directly impacted by the 9/11 attacks. An unmanned American spacecraft found ice on Mars, sparking a debate on whether life had once existed on that planet. A new generation of mobile phones let users check email, send text messages, and even get limited Web access while on the go. More than 10 million devices equipped with Wi-Fi, which allowed computers to access the Internet through radio waves instead of cables, were sold.

In 2002, an Indonesian affiliate of al Qaeda detonated two bombs at a nightclub in Bali, killing 180 people. A Gulf War veteran and his seventeen-year-old adopted son shot and killed ten victims in the greater Washington, D.C., area in a series of sniper attacks. And the U.S. economy struggled to pull out of its recession, while whistle-blowers called attention to corporate corruption.

---

### THE GLOBAL WAR

Members of the Bush administration, particularly Vice President Cheney, Donald Rumsfeld, and other Pentagon officials, had been worried about Saddam Hussein since Bush took office. The United

*With Vice President Cheney behind him, President Bush addresses Congress and the nation during his State of the Union address, January 29, 2002.*

Nations had imposed sanctions on Iraq after the Gulf War, trying to force Saddam's government to come clean about the full extent of its biological, chemical, and nuclear weapons programs and prove it had given them up. By the time Bush took office, the sanctions were weakening as international support wavered. Cheney feared Saddam was working toward weapons of mass destruction (WMD) again, threatening the Middle East and the United States.

9/11 had changed George W. Bush's view of the world. The president believed he must have a more aggressive foreign policy. "At this moment in history, if there is a world problem, we're expected to deal with it," the president told a reporter in 2002. "It's the price of power."

Bush repeatedly called this new war "the global war on terror," not a war against al Qaeda. But some foreign policy experts questioned this. Terrorism is a tactic, not a country or ideology. Was

Bush going to fight all groups that used terror? What about countries that lent support to terrorist groups, like Syria and Iran?

Because of the deadly surprise of 9/11, Bush came to believe that he could not afford to ignore potential threats. He had to stop them before the next attack. The president and his advisers began to ask, what was the biggest danger? They believed it was WMD falling into the hands of terrorists. In December, just three months after the attacks, the CIA learned that a Pakistani scientist in the country's nuclear program had met with British intelligence agents he thought were Islamist extremists and given them plans for a nuclear weapon. And the CIA had found nuclear weapon information in al Qaeda hideouts in Afghanistan.

The Bush administration feared the next intelligence failure would be a nuclear version of 9/11. Any terrorist group was a danger, and any untrustworthy government seeking weapons of mass destruction was a threat.

On January 29, 2002, Bush gave his annual State of the Union address. The country was still united after the 9/11 attacks, the war in Afghanistan appeared to be going well, and Bush enjoyed high popularity ratings. That night, he expanded the focus of the war.

"Our cause is just, and it continues. Our second goal is to prevent regimes that sponsor terror from threatening America or our friends and allies with weapons of mass destruction. North Korea is a regime arming with missiles and weapons of mass destruction, while starving its citizens. Iran aggressively pursues these weapons and exports terror, while an unelected few repress the Iranian people's hope for freedom. Iraq continues to flaunt its hostility toward America and to support terror. States like these, and their terrorist allies, constitute an axis of evil, arming to threaten the peace of the world. By seeking weapons of mass destruction, these regimes pose a grave and growing danger. We'll be deliberate, yet time is not on our side. I will not wait on events, while dangers gather."

Americans and people around the world tried to figure out what Bush's speech meant. Was it just a threat? Or did Bush mean to declare war on these three nations? What did any of these nations have to do with 9/11? "Axis" echoed the Axis powers of World War II—Nazi Germany, fascist Italy, and Imperial Japan—that had a military alliance. North Korea, Iraq, and Iran had no such alliance. In fact, Iraq and Iran were bitter enemies after having fought an inconclusive eight-year war in the eighties that killed half a million of their people. People wondered, what did any of these nations have to do with 9/11? And how ambitious was Bush's plan—would any state that sponsored terror or had a WMD program be invaded?

In reality, while Bush was warning all three countries, he was only considering war against Iraq. Since he had taken Rumsfeld aside in November, he had been meeting with the defense secretary and the general in charge of operations in the Middle East and South Asia, Tommy Franks, to review possible plans of attack. He was not committed to war, he later explained, but he wanted to be ready for it.

## PREEMPTION

While the planning continued, Bush made another key speech on June 1, this time at the U.S. Military Academy at West Point. He told the graduating cadets that 9/11 had raised the stakes. Previously, the U.S. had used containment, like the sanctions on Iraq, or deterrence, like the threat of a nuclear counterattack, to discourage attacks by enemies. That wasn't good enough anymore.

"The war on terror will not be won on the defensive," he said. "We must take the battle to the enemy, disrupt his plans and confront the worst threats before they emerge." Bush outlined a principle—preemption. The U.S. would not wait to respond until after an attack. The country would preemptively strike any enemy it believed was preparing to attack or help terrorists attack.

Colin Powell was deeply worried about all the talk in the administration of attacking Iraq. Cabinet meetings were becoming lengthy presentations of war plans by Rumsfeld. The discussions were focused on how the U.S. should attack Iraq, not why, or what the consequences would be. Powell asked the president for a meeting, so he could raise his concerns.

On August 5, Powell had dinner with Bush and National Security Advisor Condi Rice. He did not argue whether Saddam was a threat. But he raised concerns about what would happen if America invaded Iraq. America invading another Muslim country, in the heart of the Middle East, could provoke anger in the Islamic world. Oil prices could fluctuate wildly while

Iraq's large supply was out of reach during the fighting. And what would America do with Iraq after Saddam was gone? What sort of government would it build? "You are going to be the proud owner of 25 million people," he later recalled saying.

Powell urged Bush to first go to the United Nations. While the U.S. was powerful, having allies during a war would make things easier. The U.N. would send in a new team of weapons inspectors, as it had done before, to look for evidence of WMD programs. Presumably, as in the past, Saddam would not cooperate. The administration would then have a legitimate reason for action, in the international community's eyes.

## MAKING THE CASE

Cheney disagreed with Powell. He believed that the U.N. had had a decade to try and force Saddam to behave. Asking it for support might delay action while Saddam continued to build WMD. While Bush decided it was better to at least make the effort to enlist international support, Cheney pushed to make sure that the deliberations did not last long and the U.S. would move against Saddam, even if the international community ended up rejecting the idea.

On August 27, Cheney spoke at an event in Nashville, stating, "There is no doubt that Saddam Hussein now has weapons of mass destruction [and] there is no doubt he is amassing them to use against our friends, against our allies, and against us. The risks of inaction are far greater than the risk of action."

Two weeks later, on September 8, the first anniversary of the attacks on New York and Washington loomed. But the talk was about Iraq, not al Qaeda. Cheney, Powell, Rumsfeld, and Rice were all on Sunday talk shows, discussing the danger of Saddam and WMD. The *New York Times* reported, based on intelligence from the administration, that "U.S. Says Hussein Intensifies Quest for A-Bomb Parts." Rice told CNN the U.S. could not afford to wait for certain proof that Iraq had WMD. "We don't want the smoking gun to be a mushroom cloud."

It was the start of a furious lobbying campaign by the administration, an effort to convince the U.N., Congress, and the American people that war with Iraq was a necessary evil. With 9/11 ceremonies around the country marking the deaths of almost three thousand people, no one wanted to risk another attack.

Bush made his case in a speech to the U.N. General Assembly, and the Security Council began deliberations over a new resolution on Iraq. Congress began debating a bill that would give the president authority to take whatever action was necessary on Iraq—even war. The administration continued its public arguments, including the claim that a democratic Iraq could change the Middle East for the better. The theory was that many of the troubles in the Middle East—the troubles that bred support for terrorists—were due to its many corrupt, undemocratic governments. If America toppled Saddam and installed a democracy in Iraq, democratic principles would spread through the rest of the region. People in other nations would demand the same rights as Iraqis.

Bush also offered one more reason for going to war. He wanted to end the suffering of the Iraqi people. He repeatedly talked about how brutal Saddam was, how he had used chemical weapons to kill rebellious citizens—entire villages. He had killed and tortured people to stay in power for twenty-two years. Bush said the basis of his foreign policy was that, "there is a value system that cannot be compromised. And if the values are good enough for our people, they ought to be good enough for others. These are God-given values." Bush appeared to be motivated by compassion—he believed democracy was the best form of government and that an invasion would liberate the Iraqi people from Saddam's cruelty. But critics questioned why he thought it was okay for America to force democracy on a country by starting a war in which innocent people might die.

As their push continued, members of the administration sometimes went overboard with their accusations. "The Iraqi regime possesses biological and chemical weapons," Bush told reporters one day. Actually, the Intelligence Community only had evidence that they might. No one knew for sure. Bush and others also kept suggesting links between Saddam and al Qaeda—mentioning meetings between Iraqis and members of the group. Intelligence actually showed that while al Qaeda and Iraqi figures had met a few times over the years, there was no proof of an operational relationship.

But the arguments worked. Polls showed a majority of Americans supported tough action, a majority believed Saddam had weapons of mass destruction, and almost half of Americans believed Saddam was "personally involved" in 9/11.

## INTELLIGENCE ESTIMATE

What did the government actually know about Iraq, WMD, and al Qaeda? The Intelligence Community had been desperately trying to gather evidence. But none of the agencies knew much about what was going on inside Iraq. A top CIA official heading Iraq intelligence operations admitted to a reporter that the agency had just four operatives inside Iraq, and none was close to Saddam's inner circle. Because of Saddam's endless games of hide-and-seek with past U.N. inspectors, most of the evidence of Iraqi WMD programs was years old. A 2000 report from the intelligence community could only say that Saddam's government had ingredients for chemical weapons and was suspected of working toward biological weapons.

A lot of intelligence that was passed to the CIA came from Iraqis living in exile, but it was suspicious. Iraqis like Ahmed Chalabi, who headed a group called the Iraqi National Congress, supplied evidence to the U.S. because they wanted an American invasion. Chalabi also had a habit of sending his intelligence to newspaper reporters. Some people in the CIA thought Chalabi was dishonest.

The Intelligence Community felt a lot of pressure. After all, they had failed to detect the 9/11 plot. Even if they had little fresh evidence of Iraqi WMD programs, could they afford to dismiss Bush and Cheney's suspicions? Meanwhile, some officials in the Defense Department and in Cheney's office claimed the Intelligence Community was underestimating the danger. At Congress's request, the agencies composed a new National Intelligence Estimate on Iraq's WMD programs, sending the classified report to members of Congress's intelligence committees on October 2. The executive summary up front left little doubt:

> "We judge that Iraq has continued its weapons of mass destruction (WMD) programs in defiance of U.N. resolutions and restrictions. Baghdad has chemical and biological weapons as well as missiles with ranges in excess of U.N. restrictions; if left unchecked, it probably will have a nuclear weapon during this decade."

But inside the report were extensive qualifications, caveats, and doubts. People wanted absolute answers, but intelligence is rarely that solid. Still, the summary was enough proof for most readers. On October 10, the House of Representatives voted 296–133 in favor of a resolution giving Bush authority to use whatever means necessary to disarm Iraq. The Senate approved it 77–23 the next day.

The U.N. Security Council soon voted for a new resolution. The Iraqi government must submit a formal declaration of any and all WMD programs and allow inspections. On December 7, the Iraqis cooperated, sending out a twelve thousand-page report, denying that they had any weapons. Members of the administration dismissed the report as a lie. Soon afterward, the inspectors traveled to Iraq.

## OTHER PROLIFERATION CONCERNS

Back in October, the same week Congress had authorized Bush to use force against Iraq, a U.S. diplomat traveled to Pyongyang, the North Korean capital. James Kelly sat down with North Korean officials and made a damning accusation: For months the U.S. had been gathering intelligence that North Korea had been importing equipment for a uranium enrichment facility. (Uranium must be enriched to make nuclear reactor fuel or weapon fuel, usually by putting it in gas centrifuges—the facility was a second possible path to a bomb for the North Koreans.)

North Korea had bought some materials from Russia and more equipment and technology from Pakistan. But the U.S. did not know if the North Koreans had successfully assembled an enrichment facility. Members of the administration argued, however, that evidence they were importing materials meant it was time to impose tough sanctions on Kim Jong-Il's government, and hopefully bring about its collapse.

The North Koreans did not deny the intelligence. They told Kelly they had an enrichment program and then cut off any dialogue. The Bush administration began pushing countries to stop oil shipments to North Korea and urged China, North Korea's one ally and largest trading partner, to pressure Kim to change his behavior.

The proliferation issue soon became more complicated. In December, the same month that U.N. inspectors arrived in Iraq looking for evidence of a nuclear program, the media began reporting about a nuclear program next door, in Iran. An Iranian group opposed to the country's government revealed evidence of a secret uranium enrichment facility. The Iranians insisted it was only for peaceful nuclear energy purposes, but under IAEA rules, they were supposed to notify the agency of such facilities. The secrecy was suspicious.

Iran and the U.S. had not had a good relationship since the Iranian people had overthrown the Shah, a U.S.-supported monarch, in 1979. In that revolution, which brought a theocratic government of Shia Muslim clerics to power, Iranians had occupied the U.S. embassy in the capital of Tehran for more than a year, holding the Americans inside hostage. Relations with the U.S. and with Iran's Middle Eastern neighbors had not improved since, as Iran tried to export its Shia Islamist ideas. Iran had sponsored terrorist groups that had attacked Americans and Israelis. The government of Israel in particular, which had secretly developed nuclear weapons but never declared them, was opposed to any hostile country in the Middle East obtaining nuclear weapons.

Based on Iran's past behavior, there was little reason to trust that its nuclear program was truly peaceful. But Bush's Axis of Evil speech complicated international efforts to find out more about the program. Iranians who supported a less restrictive government and better relations with the West later said Bush's words gave the hardliners in the government an excuse to crush their reform efforts. What was the use of engaging with America, when it had just called Iran evil and lumped it in with its hated enemy Iraq?

## THE OTHER WAR

Most of the Afghan people had been jubilant when the Taliban were driven from power—there had not been much opposition to America's invasion because the Taliban had been so oppressive. But after decades of war, Afghanistan had no army, no experienced government officials, only the support of the international community. And Rumsfeld did not want to deploy tens of thousands of troops across a country the size of Texas to keep order until a government could be constructed. NATO troops from U.S. allies like Great Britain were deployed in Kabul, but not in the countryside.

Local warlords reasserted control. The Americans, led by CIA officers and Special Forces, gave money and other support to warlords in each region who were willing to keep order and help the Americans track down Taliban and al

Qaeda members. The warlords began collecting money the way they had before the Taliban—through the drug trade and tolls. They sent little if any money to Karzai's government.

On April 17, 2002, Bush made a speech in Virginia promising he would not forget Afghanistan. He pledged an outpouring of aid to the Afghans. But the administration did not follow up with much money. After WWII, the U.S. gave $13 billion to help rebuild Europe, equivalent to $90 billion today. At a donor's conference in Tokyo, where nations pledged money for rebuilding Afghanistan, the Bush administration pledged only $290 million. Altogether, the nations at the conference pledged $5 billion. (Iran pledged twice as much as the U.S.)

Still, there were signs democracy might take root in Afghanistan. People around the country voted for representatives to select an interim president, a new government, and a commission that would write a constitution. Karzai won the interim presidency at the meeting, but as he tried to build a national army and a government loyal to him, the warlords tried to maintain the status quo. Meanwhile, the Pentagon began to transfer troops and resources away from Afghanistan in preparation for the invasion of Iraq, and the Taliban began crossing the border from Pakistan and mounting small attacks in the south.

## THE DARK SIDE

Just five days after 9/11, Cheney had appeared on the TV show *Meet the Press*, talking about how the administration would fight back against terrorists. He said, "We have to work the dark side, if you will. Spend time in the shadows of the intelligence world. A lot of what needs to be done here will have to be done quietly, without any discussion."

America was scared after 9/11. The country had been attacked by a new sort of enemy that didn't seem to play by the rules. The CIA, the FBI, and allied foreign intelligence agencies were carrying out much of the war on terror behind the scenes, spying on suspected terrorists and sometimes capturing, imprisoning, and questioning them. The big fear was that the government would fail to prevent another attack.

"This was a war, but a different kind of war," said John Yoo, a lawyer in the White House who helped draw up rules on how the CIA and others would conduct the fight. The Bush administration would spend several years debating what tactics would be allowed in this new type of war. "We had to think through how the sets of rules . . . had to be adapted and changed to fit fighting a much different kind of enemy, a non-state actor that doesn't wear uniforms, doesn't operate in normal units, blends into civilian populations and conducts surprise attacks against civilians."

After successfully pushing the Taliban from Afghanistan and hunting for members of al Qaeda there, the Northern Alliance and the U.S. had thousands of prisoners on their hands and no idea what to do with them. Many were simply Taliban foot soldiers, paid to pick up a gun. Some were al Qaeda members who might have valuable information. Some in the administration felt that because al Qaeda was a terrorist group, not an army, past rules governing prisoner treatment did not apply. And because the Taliban were allied with al Qaeda, many in the administration made no distinction between the two.

The administration developed several tactics for imprisoning and interrogating captives. Many, including low-level Taliban and al Qaeda members, were imprisoned at the U.S. Naval base in Guantanamo Bay, Cuba. The administration claimed American law did not apply there. Detainees could be held indefinitely, without access to lawyers, and without the rights they would have had under U.S. laws. Some suspected al Qaeda members were handed over to allies like Egypt and Morocco, whose foreign intelligence services had no rules against torture. Any information the foreign interrogators obtained was given to the U.S. More high-level prisoners were held in CIA-operated prisons in foreign countries such as Thailand and Poland. And after a lengthy debate within the administration, the White House allowed U.S. interrogators to use some techniques that had previously been considered torture. The administration believed such techniques were the only way to protect the country. None of this was made public.

# 2003

## *Mission Accomplished*

IN 2003, AMERICANS spent more than $57 million on cellular phone ringtones, up from $16 million in 2002. A Harvard sophomore created a new Web site one February night, facemash.com, that compared pictures of fellow students so people could vote on who was more attractive. The next semester he adapted it into a more advanced site called Facebook. Americans tuned in to a reality show called *Joe Millionaire*, where women competed for the affections of a multimillionaire, only to find out he was actually poor.

In 2003, the Space Shuttle *Columbia* disintegrated while reentering the earth's atmosphere, killing all seven astronauts on board. A new virus called Severe Acute Respiratory Syndrome (SARS) quickly spread around the world. On New Year's Day, the North Korean government ordered IAEA inspectors to leave the country as the Koreans began removing spent nuclear fuel rods (and potential weapon fuel) from their reactor. In a region of Sudan called Darfur, rebel groups challenged the government, which responded by sending in militia groups called Janjaweed, who systematically terrorized the local population, killing innocents and driving 600,000 refugees away from their homes.

---

### WMD

Since November of 2001, Rumsfeld had been pushing General Tommy Franks to rethink the plans he would use if the U.S. invaded Iraq. Rumsfeld believed the days of big ground assaults led by tank units and large numbers of ground troops were over. Afghanistan gave him a model. Air power and a limited number of troops had successfully forced the Taliban out of power.

Iraq was a different enemy. Unlike the Toyota pickup-truck-equipped Taliban, Saddam Hussein had a 400,000-man army, complete with large tank divisions. And there was no local ally like the Northern Alliance. An American ground assault was needed. But Rumsfeld still believed the military's original plan for a 350,000-soldier invasion was outdated—America's superiority in technology meant it could beat a larger force. He pushed Franks and his advisers relentlessly to streamline. Eventually, the plan would call for only 145,000 soldiers.

There was some griping in the Pentagon that it wasn't enough, but Deputy Secretary of Defense Paul Wolfowitz told Congress that it would be sufficient because troops would be "greeted as liberators" by the Iraqis. Once Saddam was driven from power, Iraqis would support the Americans, eliminating the need for a large occupying force.

A majority of Americans supported military action. A *Time* magazine poll in February found that 72 percent of Americans thought war was justified because it "will help eliminate weapons of mass destruction in Iraq." But most people worldwide opposed war. To many nations, the world's superpower launching a preemptive attack on another country seemed like a dangerous precedent. Whom would the U.S. invade next?

In many Muslim nations, Bush's plan to attack another Islamic nation after the invasion of Afghanistan led some to believe the president was deliberately targeting the Muslim world. Many Middle Easterners were still unsure about the 9/11 attacks—wild conspiracy theories abounded that the attacks were actually the work of the CIA or of Israeli spies, part of a plot to give the U.S. an excuse to conquer the Muslim world.

Bush had made his decision, though. On March 17, he gave Saddam and his sons Uday and Qusay forty-eight hours to leave Iraq, or the U.S. would act.

## REGIME CHANGE

Three days after Bush's ultimatum to Saddam, American bombers and missiles struck a farm belonging to him, near his hometown of Tikrit. But the dictator was not there. The U.S. had acted on bad intelligence.

Later that same day, while planes dropped bombs on Baghdad, ground troops, including some British units, headed into southern Iraq from Kuwait. Special Forces moved into the west and the north. American units moved up the Euphrates River toward Baghdad, fighting Saddam's army.

General Franks's plan relied on speed, but the quick advance obscured some problems. Few troops were left behind to secure areas in the rear and protect supply lines. And the Americans soon discovered that not all of Saddam's forces wore uniforms. Units known as Fedayeen blended in with the population, attacked the Americans when least expected, and often hit the more vulnerable units—supply convoys manned by Army Reserve or National Guard soldiers.

The strongest divisions of the Iraqi army were defeated outside Baghdad. By April 3, the U.S. Army had taken Baghdad's airport. On the seventh, they took control of Saddam's palace complex in the heart of the city. The Iraqi dictator had already fled. On the ninth, Iraqis, with American troops' help, tore down a statue of Saddam in a Baghdad square and celebrated their freedom. It was broadcast around the world. Bush's popularity in the U.S., which had hit 92 percent after 9/11, but settled into the high 50s, shot back up to 77 percent.

But the jubilation in Iraq quickly turned to chaos. Some Iraqis, after decades of watching Saddam and his corrupt political organization, the Baath party, steal from them and make life miserable, began looting every government facility they could—even museums. Plumbing pipes were stripped from some buildings.

There were just two U.S. brigades—about 5,000 soldiers—patrolling the streets of Baghdad, a city of 5 million people. And they had orders to guard against Iraqi soldiers or Fedayeen, not to act as policemen. So the looting continued.

At a Pentagon briefing, when asked about the chaos, Rumsfeld was dismissive. "Stuff happens. Freedom's untidy, and free people are free to make mistakes." But the looting quickly made it apparent that the U.S. did not have a strategy for restoring order. The war plan called for another 100,000 to 150,000 troops to move in once Baghdad fell. But Rumsfeld questioned that—Why would it take more troops to occupy the country than to defeat Saddam's army? In the end, most of the additional troops were not deployed.

Very little of the prewar planning had been devoted to what would happen once Saddam fell. Just two months before the invasion, Rumsfeld had hired a retired general, Jay Garner, to supervise reconstruction. Garner arrived in Baghdad with few resources and few instructions—there was little he could do to stop the chaos. After only two weeks on the job, Rumsfeld effectively fired him, saying that a new presidential envoy was coming to Iraq to take over.

## RECIPE FOR TROUBLE

On May 1, President Bush, a former Air National Guard pilot, donned a flight suit and took the copilot seat in a navy jet. The pilot flew for most of the trip, but Bush did take the controls for a short time. The jet landed on the aircraft carrier USS *Abraham Lincoln* near the coast of California. Bush changed into a suit, strode out on the deck, and gave an address to the assembled sailors and the American public, announcing, "major combat operations in Iraq have ended." Bush told the servicemen and -women, "Because of you, our nation is more secure. Because of you, the tyrant has fallen and Iraq is free." Behind him hung a large banner that read "Mission Accomplished." Meanwhile, Franks told his commanders to be ready to withdraw from Iraq by September—all but 30,000 troops would leave by then.

The new man in charge of reconstruction, Paul Bremer, was a respected former diplomat and counterterrorism expert, but he was not a Middle East specialist and did not speak Arabic. When Bremer accepted the job, he had two weeks to prepare before he went to Baghdad. He arrived on May 12. "We flew on the C-130 into Baghdad. The thing that was striking to us was the fact that a lot of the buildings were on fire," said Bremer later. Many buildings had been burning for a month because there was no fire department—all the firefighters had disappeared, much like the police.

Bremer's first order after taking control was to ban any senior members of Saddam's Baath party from government work. He felt Iraq must make a clean start. But once the order was carried out, there were no experienced Iraqis to run key ministries. The order eliminated the jobs of an estimated 75,000 people.

On May 23, Bremer dissolved the almost 400,000-man Iraqi army and the Interior ministry, another 285,000 people, including all police officers. Garner's aides had been meeting with Iraqi generals, dis-

*From the deck of the USS* Abraham Lincoln *off the coast of San Diego, the president tells the country that "major combat operations" in Iraq are over, May 1, 2003.*

cussing keeping the Iraqi army intact and putting soldiers to work at reconstruction. Suddenly more than half a million people, many of whom had guns, were unemployed.

Within days, anti-American demonstrations began in Baghdad. Clerics made anti-American statements during their Friday sermons in the mosques. Iraqis had held mixed feelings about the invasion—most were happy to see Saddam fall, but felt shame about being occupied. Now many started to grumble: When would the Americans leave? When would the electricity in Baghdad be restored? Soon, American troops encountered small-scale attacks.

An insurgency was developing—Iraqi public opinion was turning against the Americans, which meant U.S. and coalition troops would receive no support from the population in preventing attacks or finding the perpetrators. Some Baath party leaders had escaped to Syria and were organizing attacks, sending in money and fighters. And Arabs around the region

*An Iraqi girl watches soldiers from the 82nd Airborne Division conduct a sweep in Baghdad, November 30, 2003. They were looking for bomb-making material belonging to insurgents.*

were starting to send money to support this insurgency.

Back in Washington, Rumsfeld dismissed these attacks as the last gasp of a few Saddam loyalists. Bush was as dismissive as Rumsfeld: "There are some who feel . . . that they can attack us there. My answer is this: Bring it on."

On August 7, they did. A car bomb exploded outside the Jordanian embassy in Baghdad, killing eleven people. On the nineteenth, a cement truck loaded with explosives rammed into the wall of the United Nations mission in Baghdad. That killed twenty-two people. The U.N. responded by withdrawing most of its staff in Iraq, cutting from eight hundred people to fifteen. The insurgents went after international organizations, aid groups, and U.S. allies in the coalition. They wanted to drive them out so the Americans were left alone and reconstruction was slowed. They also attacked Iraqi police stations, hoping to discourage Iraqis from taking jobs in the new police force. No cops meant no security for average citizens.

The insurgents also attacked Shi'ite leaders. The majority of Iraq's population belongs to one of three major ethnic/religious groups: Shi'ite Arabs, who make up about 60 percent of the population; Sunni Kurds, who make up about 18 percent; and Sunni Arabs, who make up only about 18 percent but had controlled Iraq's government for much of the past century. With the U.S. planning on installing a democratic government, the Sunni Arabs had the most to lose. The majority of the insurgents were Sunni Arabs.

The insurgents' weapon of choice was the improvised explosive device (IED), a small bomb, usually placed by the side of the road and detonated when a U.S. patrol drove by. It was unpredictable and deadly. The best defense against the bombs was for civilians to warn the Americans about them, but as the public grew resentful over the U.S. presence, they stopped coming forward. Any hope of building trust between U.S. troops and Iraqi civilians was rapidly disappearing.

## TRUST DAMAGED

The war was also straining trust at home. As casualties began to rise, many Americans began to ask, Where were the weapons of mass destruction? The WMD experts were finding nothing.

Although the administration urged patience, all the Intelligence Community's doubts and caveats on the intelligence from before the war began emerging. In early July, a former ambassador named Joe Wilson wrote an op-ed piece in the *New York Times* objecting to a claim Bush had made in his State of the Union Address in January. While making the case that Saddam sought nuclear weapons, Bush had mentioned a British intelligence report stating that Iraqi officials had tried to buy uranium from the African nation of Niger.

During the buildup to war, Cheney's office had asked the CIA to investigate this claim. Cheney was convinced Iraq had a nuclear program and wanted proof. The CIA sent Wilson to Niger. He investigated, found proof that the story was false, and reported back. But Cheney's office still believed the story. They ignored Wilson's discoveries, and several officials mentioned the story to the press.

Given Wilson's op-ed and the unsuccessful search for WMD, people now began to reexamine the intelligence that had led to the Iraq war. If the government's claim that Iraq had enriched uranium was wrong, what other intelligence had Bush administration officials presented as solid fact that was really only speculation? Had the U.S. really had adequate reason to go to war?

## GETTING TOUGH

The debate over whether America should have gone to war meant little to the soldiers actually in Iraq. They were there. And their frustration was growing, as insurgents continued to hit them with IEDs and other random attacks. In May, thirty-seven Americans were killed. In July, another forty-seven died.

The number of deaths was not high compared to previous wars, but the attacks were wounding many more soldiers. In May, 54 were wounded; in July, it was 226. By October, it was 413. American body armor, helmets, and battlefield medical care were all more advanced than in past conflicts. That saved lives. But soldiers who might have died in the past still had dreadful injuries—amputations, brain injuries, or psychological damage. Even soldiers who were not physically hurt were mentally scarred.

The military's biggest challenge that summer was that it had little intelligence on the insurgents. They could not find out who they were and when they would strike. Soldiers began trying to find out by conducting sweeps in villages and neighborhoods across Iraq. They would arrest anyone they suspected of helping the insurgency. In some cases, units would arrest almost every man under forty in a village.

These raids involved soldiers entering homes by force, making the entire family sit down on the ground, and searching the house for evidence. The young men were handcuffed and taken away for questioning. Iraq is a very traditional society—entering someone's home and ordering the men around or pushing them down and handcuffing them in front of their wives and children is considered a horrible insult. Many men, once released by the coalition forces, felt they had to seek revenge to regain their honor.

Once the units rounded up suspects, they questioned them back at base. Many were then sent to a detention camp for further questioning. The original invasion plan had not called for a large detention system. So that summer, the military reopened Abu Ghraib prison. Many Iraqis were upset by this—Abu Ghraib had been one of Saddam's most notorious prisons, where people were tortured for opposing the government.

By late fall, there were more than ten thousand detainees at the prison. Military intelligence estimated that 90 percent were either innocent or unimportant. But determining who was a legitimate prisoner and who just got caught up in sweeps proved to be a slow task. Innocent men were held for months.

Rumsfeld grew frustrated at the lack of intelligence the military was getting from the detainees. So he allowed military intelligence officers to use some of the same interrogation techniques on Iraqi detainees that Guantanamo Bay officers used on suspected al Qaeda members, techniques that many people considered torture.

## THE MASTERMIND

The administration's focus on Iraq did not mean the campaign against al Qaeda had ended. On March 1, 2003, an informant in Pakistan sneaked into a bathroom and sent a text message: "I am with K.S.M." A few hours later, American and Pakistani forces raided the house and found their target—Khalid Sheikh Mohammed, the chief planner of the 9/11 attacks. Mohammed was quickly placed on a plane and flown to a secret CIA prison in Poland. He asked for a lawyer. That request was ignored.

For over a year, the CIA questioned Mohammed, using many of the enhanced interrogation techniques approved by the White House. Mohammed gladly took credit for 9/11 and claimed to be responsible for several other attacks. He provided a lot of valuable intelligence. He also provided false information. It's unknown whether Mohammed would have refused to talk, or would have been more cooperative, if he hadn't been subjected to the enhanced interrogation techniques.

## WE GOT HIM

At a December 14 press conference in Baghdad, Bremer told reporters, "We got him." An informant had told American soldiers that someone important was hiding on a farm south of Tikrit. On the thirteenth, in an orange grove under a primitive trap door, soldiers found Saddam Hussein hiding in a hole. He quickly surrendered.

Many commanders believed Saddam's capture would lead to the end of the insurgency, as Iraqis saw that Saddam was not going to retake the country. And in fact, over the next three months, Iraqis started to give Americans better intelligence and many insurgents surrendered. After nine months in Iraq, there was hope the fighting might soon be over.

# 2004

## *Truthiness*

IN 2004, THE Boston Red Sox broke a curse and won the World Series for the first time in eighty-six years. *Mean Girls*, starring Lindsay Lohan and Tina Fey, was a box office hit. In March, a group of Muslims in Spain attacked commuter trains in Madrid with coordinated bombings that killed 191 people. Palestinian Authority Chairman Yasser Arafat, the leading figure in the Palestinian liberation movement since the sixties, died.

In 2004, red state and blue state America reemerged. The spirit that had united the country after the 9/11 attacks faded, replaced by the same partisanship that marked the 2000 election. If anything the partisan divide was worse because the stakes were higher—there was not just a presidential election, there were also two wars.

---

### THE WAR HERO

Democrats who were against the Iraq war had been growing more vocal for months, and the approaching Democratic presidential primaries only increased their passion. Republicans were passionate too, but about reelecting Bush and showing support for the war. It was a marked difference from 2000, when many thought the election did not matter.

In January, as candidates crisscrossed Iowa stumping for the caucuses, many Democrats believed that their leaders had given in to Bush too much. The Democratic activists were now demanding that party leaders compromise less. Their number one priority was ending the Iraq war.

These activists were more organized and mobilized than before, which made their voices louder. They believed Republicans had been better at grassroots organization—raising cash and turning out their voters—in recent elections and vowed to learn from that. One of the biggest tools for members of both parties was the Internet. Blogs like Daily Kos became important forums for people to share their ideas, find fellow activists, and organize fundraising and campaign activities. Organizations like MoveOn.org used the Web to raise money for candidates who shared their members' beliefs.

The candidate who best tapped the Internet as a source for support during the primary season was Howard Dean. A doctor and former governor of Vermont, Dean was considered an underdog in the buildup to the primaries. Most of his opponents, who were senators and congressmen, had voted in favor of authorizing the Iraq invasion. (Since he was a governor, Dean had not had to make that decision in 2002, when a majority of the country still supported war.) Dean said the war was wrong and a mistake. He became known for fiery speeches. Thanks to loyal supporters on the Internet who called themselves Deaniacs, he took the lead in fundraising and endorsements before the Iowa caucuses in late January.

But Iowa Democrats are more conservative, and they ignored the many young volunteers who came to the state to urge people to support Dean. He came in third, finishing behind Massachusetts Senator John Kerry and North Carolina Senator John Edwards. Internet activists had not yet figured out how to translate online support into get-out-the-vote efforts.

A week later, in New Hampshire, Kerry won again. As spring approached, Kerry won most other states and soon locked up the nomination.

The Massachusetts senator was the opposite of Dean. He was not the most exciting speaker—he had an unusual talent for using thirty words when three would do. But Kerry had a compelling life story. After college he enlisted in the navy, became an officer, and was sent to Vietnam in 1968. Commanding a small fifty-foot-long vessel called a swift boat that patrolled rivers in South Vietnam, Kerry earned multiple medals for bravery and for his wounds during several dangerous missions.

After his tour of duty, he became an outspoken opponent of the war. He testified before Congress, condemning the

*Jon Stewart (right) interviews presidential candidate John Kerry on* The Daily Show, *August 24, 2004.*

war and saying it had led soldiers to commit "atrocities" against the Vietnamese people. Kerry believed he was condemning the government of Richard Nixon for continuing the war. But some veterans felt Kerry had betrayed them, serving with them and then saying they were fighting "for a mistake."

During nineteen years in the Senate, Kerry built a reputation as a leader on foreign policy and military affairs. Democrats were tired of being accused of being soft on terrorism and national security by Republicans. They believed Kerry, with his expertise and his record as a war hero, could take on Bush.

## LOSING HEARTS AND MINDS

After nearly nine months in Iraq, the Americans tasked with finding weapons of mass destruction in Iraq had to accept that they would not find any. On January 23, David Kay, head of the Iraq Survey Group, said that Saddam Hussein had fooled the world—not by hiding WMD programs, but by ending them without telling anyone. Asked about the stockpiles, Kay told a Senate committee, "I don't think they existed." Kay believed that under U.N. pressure, Saddam had ended the programs, but refused to allow the U.N. to confirm this because he feared Iran would attack Iraq if it thought he no longer had weapons.

The U.S. military had hoped the capture of Saddam in late 2003 would mark the beginning of the end for the insurgency. But opposition to U.S. presence in Iraq went beyond those loyal to Saddam—more and more Iraqis were growing hostile to the U.S. presence. Basic services and security were still nonexistent, and U.S. soldiers continued their indiscriminate sweeps. The number of attacks continued to rise in the first half of 2004.

Because there were not enough U.S. troops in Iraq, units could not maintain a constant presence in towns and villages. Once they had chased the insurgents out of an area and made alliances with local leaders, the Americans usually had to leave for another town. Then the insurgents returned and killed the tribal elders who had helped the Americans.

## ENHANCED DETENTION

On April 28, the CBS news show *60 Minutes* broadcast a report on abuse of Iraqi detainees at Abu Ghraib prison. The *New Yorker* followed up with a more extensive report, including an army investigation. Several members of a reserve military police unit from Maryland, assigned to act as prison guards at Abu Ghraib, had abused Iraqi prisoners from October through December of 2003—and they had taken pictures.

Bush had said America would liberate Iraqis from Saddam's tyranny. But prisoners were ritually humiliated by America at the same prison where Saddam had tortured people. In Iraq, where personal honor meant everything, these humiliating photos were an invaluable recruiting tool for insurgents and badly damaged American credibility with both Iraqis and the world.

The MPs claimed they were just softening up the detainees for interrogation as ordered. While they undoubtedly went beyond their instructions, the enhanced interrogation programs Rumsfeld had established created a fuzzy line between interrogation and torture.

## GETTING SWIFT-BOATED

The missteps in Iraq were impacting the presidential campaign—it was the biggest issue in the race. In January, a poll found that a quarter of Americans believed the war was going badly. By May, the number had risen to 51 percent.

A month earlier, a new political organization had introduced itself to the press with little fanfare. Swift Boat Veterans for Truth was a group of Vietnam vets who had served on fast attack boats, as Kerry had. Many had long disliked him, believing that his Vietnam protests had been a betrayal of their service during the war. But rather than attacking Kerry for his antiwar protests, they decided it would be more effective to question whether he had really earned his medals.

The media did not pay much attention when the Swift Boat Vets announced their campaign. After all, Kerry's heroism in Vietnam was well documented. Few stories would appear in national newspapers or magazines about the organization until August. But the Swift Boat Vets did not need the major media outlets. They began a sophisticated public relations campaign focused on an audience predisposed to believe their message—right-wing talk radio.

Talk radio had been a growing medium for reaching conservative listeners for a decade. Charismatic hosts like Rush Limbaugh would analyze the news of the day with a strong conservative slant. Helped by a PR consultant, various Swift Boat Vets went on multiple radio shows a day, repeating their charges against Kerry and urging listeners to go to the Swift Boat Vets Web site. It was another instance of using the Web for political organizing, and it worked. As the Swift Boat Vets gained attention in conservative circles, they attracted money from wealthy donors and were able to start running TV ads against Kerry.

## TRUTHINESS

The Swift Boat Vets' use of conservative talk radio illustrated how much the media had changed, even since the 2000 election. The Internet and other technologies allowed for the flow of so much more information. Americans once got their news from their local newspaper and the three network news broadcasts. Cable TV news channels took off during the nineties, and by the 2000 election, there was a channel that purposefully targeted conservative viewers—Fox News. (In 2008, MSNBC would go in the opposite direction, airing more shows with a liberal slant.) Satellite radio offered even more options. And 2004 was the year of the blogs, which became a major source of election information for the first time. Many blogs had a liberal or a conservative slant.

The most popular TV "news" show that year was on cable's Comedy Central. *The Daily Show* was actually a parody of news shows. Hosted by comedian Jon Stewart, it poked fun at the posturing, incompetence, and hypocrisy of political figures. The show had first become a hit during the 2000 election, but it attracted more than a million viewers a night during the 2004 campaign.

In 2004, a conservative could read conservative blogs like Power Line, watch Fox News, and listen to talk radio, all of which would be focused on key stories that appealed to conservatives—like the Swift Boat Vets' attacks on Kerry. A liberal could watch PBS's *NewsHour* and read the *New York Times* and liberal blogs like Daily Kos online. Neither had to listen to a single viewpoint they didn't agree with. While the new media gave people more information than ever before, it also encouraged partisanship.

And it may have obscured the truth. Naval records and eyewitness accounts say that most of the claims made by the Swift Boat Vets were false. Only one of the Swift Boat Vets had actually served on one of Kerry's boats. But as the vets made their charges on talk radio and conservative bloggers began writing about it, enough of a buzz was created that more mainstream media outlets began writing or doing segments on the controversy. And in conservative circles, the false charges became accepted fact.

That was one of the side effects of this fragmented media—while Republicans and Democrats used to hold different opinions on things, now many actually believed a different set of "facts" that they wished were true. Some Democrats believed George W. Bush had used 9/11 as an excuse to attack Iraq because he wanted access to its oil. Some Republicans believed John Kerry wanted to surrender in Iraq and let the United Nations control American foreign policy. How could conservatives and liberals work together on problems when their basic facts came from different realities?

It wouldn't be coined for another year, but there was a term for this: Truthiness. It was introduced by Stephen Colbert, a *Daily Show* correspondent who got his own show, *The Colbert Report*, in

2005. *Merriam-Webster's Dictionary* called "truthiness" the word of the year in 2006. "We're not talking about truth, we're talking about something that seems like truth—the truth we want to exist," Colbert told viewers. He would later tell an interviewer, "Truthiness is tearing apart our country. It used to be everyone was entitled to their own opinion, but not their own facts. But that's not the case anymore. Facts matter not at all. Perception is everything."

## UNFIT FOR COMMAND

Even though the Swift Boat Vets' attacks were truthiness, they were getting plenty of attention by August. Some voters began to wonder: Had Kerry been honest about his Vietnam heroics? Kerry did not help himself—his campaign responded slowly to the Swift Boat attacks, convinced no one would believe false accusations.

The Bush campaign had a two-prong strategy. They wanted to stress that Bush was a bold leader who had taken action after 9/11 and would continue to take bold action to protect the country. The second prong was portraying Kerry as a weak leader who would not be able to keep America safe, and whose opposition to the war in Iraq meant surrender in the war on terror.

While the polls would stay close until Election Day, this time the result was clear by the next morning. Bush won 50.7 percent of the popular vote on November 2, while Kerry won 48.3 percent. Bush won the electoral college 286 to 251. And voters' passion translated into a high turnout. American University's Center for the Study of the American Electorate reported a record turnout of 60.7 percent of eligible voting-age citizens, 6.4 percent higher than in 2000 and the highest since 1968.

While not a landslide, it was a more decisive victory for Bush than in 2000. The difference? One was turnout—the Republicans were better at getting their voters to the polls on Election Day. Another was moderate voters, who ranked security as their top issue. These voters may not have been as conservative as Bush, but they trusted him more than Kerry to protect them.

## REFERENDUM

There was another issue on the ballot in many states that Election Day—same-sex marriage. Gay rights is a sensitive issue in America. Homosexuals had been fighting for civil rights since the sixties, and were more culturally accepted by many Americans than ever before. But they wanted the right to marry each other, which many Americans did not agree they should have.

Marriage was more than a symbolic issue for gays. Married couples share a lot of legal rights, from the right to visit each other in the hospital and make medical decisions for each other to deductions on taxes or health insurance costs.

To supporters, both gay and straight, same-sex marriage was a personal issue between the two people who wanted to enter into marriage. It was a symbol of love. To opponents, it was a religious issue. Christianity (like many other religions) defines marriage as being between a man and a woman and forbids homosexuality.

In 2003, the Massachusetts Supreme Court ruled that state laws banning same-sex marriage were unconstitutional. Gay couples immediately began traveling to Massachusetts to get married. Other states said they would not recognize the marriages legally. In February of 2004, San Francisco's mayor announced his city would begin issuing same-sex marriage licenses, ignoring a state law banning them.

Conservatives fought back, arguing that courts were overruling the will of the majority. They proposed ballot referenda to ban same-sex marriage in several states. On election day, all eleven states with referenda passed them, by large majorities.

## THE WAVE

On December 26, as the world prepared for another New Year, an earthquake occurred under the Indian Ocean, the second largest ever recorded. The quake set off a massive tsunami, a tidal wave that crashed onto shores all over South Asia, from India to Sri Lanka to Thailand to Indonesia. Many people were caught unaware as a wall of water plowed into their towns. Almost 230,000 people died.

Countries around the world sent an incredible outpouring of aid, eventually totaling $7 billion. They also sent volunteers to help in rescue and recovery. The tsunami was a grim end to the year. It was a reminder that Mother Nature could be unpredictable. But it also showed that in the new globalized world, aid and help could flow fast to disaster-struck areas. Everyone on the planet was connected.

# 2005

## *A Deluge of Problems*

IN 2005, LANCE Armstrong won an unprecedented seventh straight Tour de France bicycle race, and announced he would retire. Columbia Records signed the Jonas Brothers to a recording contract. It was the worst Atlantic hurricane season in the one hundred fifty-four years that records had been kept, with twenty-eight named tropical storms and four Category 5 storms (the most intense). In the U.S., gas prices rose steadily, eventually exceeding $3 a gallon—more in some locations.

In 2005, an Iraqi court put Saddam Hussein on trial. Congress and President Bush intervened in a legal struggle over a Florida woman who had been in a vegetative state for fifteen years—her husband believed she would have wanted to end life support, while her parents disagreed—and many Republicans rushed to support them. Israel began withdrawing all settlers and troops from the Gaza Strip, leaving it under the control of the Palestinian Authority, but without any formal treaty. On July 7, four British Muslim men detonated bombs on the London public transit system, killing fifty-six people.

### FREEDOM IS ON THE MARCH

"I want this to be the freedom speech," President Bush told his speechwriter when they began discussing plans for his second Inaugural Address. And it would be—when Bush addressed the crowd from the Capitol on January 20, he used the words *free*, *freedom*, and *liberty* forty-nine times.

Starting his second term, Bush had something he hadn't had four years earlier: a clear mandate. The election had been close, but there was no recount, no lost popular vote. Armed with his victory, Bush wanted to announce a bold foreign policy agenda—a freedom agenda. "The survival of liberty in our land increasingly depends on the success of liberty in other lands," he said. "The best hope for peace in our world is the expansion of freedom in all the world."

Bush was saying that the best method for preventing future attacks like 9/11 was for the U.S. to spread democracy around the globe. His government's goal would be to promote freedom and to support those who campaign for human rights.

It was a big change from the man who originally took office promising to intervene overseas only when American interests were directly threatened. Many observers asked, What did Bush plan to do to implement this idea? While freedom and democracy were noble goals, didn't events in Iraq prove that attempting to spread freedom by force was a risky endeavor? Some nations, like China, continued to question whether America's version of freedom was the best. Others asked, would Bush challenge dictators who were helping him in the war on terror but repressing their own people?

Certainly there were examples to back up Bush's assertion that freedom was "on the march." A month earlier, protestors in Ukraine had demonstrated after it appeared a presidential runoff election had been stolen for the ruling prime minister. After three days of rallies, the Ukranian Supreme Court ordered a new election, and opposition candidate Viktor Yushchenko won. In March, opposition leaders in Kyrgyzstan protested longtime President Askar Akayev's rigging of parliamentary elections, forcing him to flee the country.

And in Lebanon, a wave of demonstrations pushed Syria to withdraw its troops there. Syria had moved soldiers into Lebanon two decades earlier, during Lebanon's civil war. Many Lebanese opposed the presence of a foreign army. In February, former prime minister Rafik Hariri, an outspoken opponent of Syria, died in a suicide bombing. Syria's government became the prime suspect in the bombing. A month of protests and international condemnation of the attack convinced Syria to withdraw their soldiers a month later.

There was debate in the United States—were these movements around the world an effect of Bush's effort to establish democracy in Iraq? Some observers believed they were. Others said they were a sign of how globalization and technology had empowered ordinary people. It was harder for governments to repress their subjects when the Internet and satellite TV gave the people access to a world of ideas and supporters.

Bush could take direct credit for two democratic events. In January, the people of Iraq participated in their first free election since the invasion, as they went to the polls to approve a special assembly that would draft a new constitution. And in October 2004, Hamid Karzai had won a full term as president of Afghanistan in the country's first election in decades.

But there was also plenty of evidence that democracy was not going to sweep the planet just because Bush had made it official policy. Governments around the world, even America's allies, were still going to do what was in their own best interests. And there were clear signs that Bush's decision to invade Iraq and the missteps that followed had eroded America's influence in the world. Allies were less willing to go along with American policies, and enemies felt empowered—with America bogged down in Iraq and Afghanistan, Bush wasn't going to invade another country any time soon.

## THE PYGMY

Bush desperately wanted democracy to spread to North Korea and topple Kim Jong-Il's government. He hated the dictator and the way Kim treated North Korean citizens. Bush once referred to Kim as "the pygmy" in front of senators, implying he was a small, second-rate man. There was hope in the administration that the invasion of Iraq would send a message to Kim—reform or you might be next.

But with the U.S. facing a tougher fight than expected in Iraq and failing to find WMD, Kim apparently decided that Saddam's big mistake had been not actually having WMD. In January of 2004, he invited an American delegation of nuclear experts to visit his reactor, and his scientists showed one of the visitors a small sample of plutonium they had apparently manufactured. It was proof they could create fuel for a nuclear bomb. On February 10, 2005, North Korea announced it had developed a nuclear weapon because it felt threatened by the United States.

The Bush administration seemed to have little leverage for negotiating an end to North Korea's nuclear program. In fact, Bush refused to even negotiate directly with the North Koreans—administration officials felt it would give

Kim what he wanted, to be treated like a world power, a nation on the same level as the United States. They insisted all talks be among the six nations with the most direct interests in the problem—North Korea, the U.S., South Korea, Japan, China, and Russia. The U.S. offered nothing that would actually induce North Korea to give up its weapons programs. So the standoff continued.

## MAHMOUD

The other nation the U.S. worried about when it came to nuclear proliferation was Iran. In November 2004, the U.K., France, and Germany announced an agreement with Iran—the Iranian government would suspend uranium enrichment while negotiations over the future of its nuclear program continued. But the Europeans were frustrated because the U.S. refused to get involved in the discussions—again, the Bush administration refused to talk directly with Iran because it did not want to appear to be legitimizing its government.

The White House hoped that Iran's presidential election in June would give them a new leader to negotiate with. Even though Supreme Leader Ayatollah Ali Khamenei and his fellow Shia clerics held the real power in Iran, the president was the head of the day-to-day government and would be the one to do any negotiating.

*Mahmoud Ahmadinejad, president of the Islamic Republic of Iran, addresses the United Nations General Assembly on September 17, 2005, three months after his surprise election win.*

When the results of the election were announced, the world was surprised. Mahmoud Ahmadinejad, the mayor of Tehran and a little-known ultraconservative, had won. Ahmadinejad had appealed to poor and rural Iranians by promising to improve the economy. He was also supported by many conservative clerics and the Revolutionary Guards, a powerful ideological branch of the Iranian military, dedicated to protecting the revolution.

Ahmadinejad was not an ideal negotiating partner. He was the only presidential candidate who had spoken out against talks with the United States. After the election, he gave a speech calling Israel a "disgraceful stain [on] the Islamic world," adding that, "Soon this stain of disgrace will be cleaned from the garment of the world of Islam, and this is attainable." Was Ahmadinejad hinting that Iran would develop nuclear weapons and try to destroy Israel? He denied it, but it was one of several occasions when Ahmadinejad would make anti-Israel or anti-Semitic remarks.

Ahmadinejad seemed to take a sort of pleasure in provoking the U.S. and the international community. Perhaps he thought it increased support for him among his people and other Muslims. He was also a forceful proponent of Iran's nuclear program. He maintained it was peaceful and it was Iran's right as a free nation—giving it up would mean subservience to the West.

In August, Ahmadinejad effectively killed the talks with the Europeans, announcing Iran was producing more centrifuges. It appeared Iran was emulating North Korea, trying to obtain nuclear weapons while the world debated what to do.

The Bush administration responded by asking the U.N. Security Council for sanctions against Iran. But China and Russia opposed the idea. Their governments said there was no proof Iran had a weapons program, and that the U.S. intelligence suggesting it did was from the same analysts who had claimed Iraq had WMD. Bush's mistakes and struggles in Iraq were affecting his other foreign policies.

## ATOMIC ALLY

North Korea and Iran were nations in different regions, with weapons programs in very different stages. But they had one thing in common—they both had atomic weapons programs thanks to Pakistan, a nation that was supposed to be one of America's closest allies in the war on terror.

In the summer of 2003, U.S. forces had seized a ship heading for Libya loaded with parts for nuclear weapon production. Confronted with the evidence, Libya admitted to having a nuclear program. Officials told the U.S. they were sourcing parts and know-how from Pakistan, and specifically from Dr. Abdul Qadeer Khan.

Khan was a hero in Pakistan for his role in developing a Pakistani nuclear program. India had conducted a nuclear test

# DIFFERENT PRIORITIES

The Khan episode showed that almost four years after Pakistan agreed to cooperate with America in the war on terror, American and Pakistani goals were still far apart. Even though Musharraf had seized power in a coup—hardly a model of Bush's freedom agenda—Bush needed the Pakistani leader to help him fight the Taliban and al Qaeda; Pakistan needed American financial aid. So the two countries shared some common interests.

But their goals for the government of Afghanistan were very different. America wanted a strong government in Afghanistan, which meant it supported the Karzai administration. Pakistan's government, however, worried that a strong Karzai administration would ally itself with India, Pakistan's enemy. America asked Pakistan to position its army along its border with Afghanistan to hunt for Taliban and al Qaeda members, but Pakistan kept most of its forces on the Indian border.

When America's ambassador to Afghanistan left the country in 2005, he commented that Pakistani journalists had recently interviewed a senior Taliban leader in Pakistan. "If a TV station can get in touch with them, how can [the Inter-Services Intelligence], the intelligence service of a country which has nuclear bombs and a lot of security and military forces, not find them?" He was implying that Pakistan was giving Taliban leaders sanctuary.

Pakistan angrily denied this. Musharraf kept reassuring Bush that the ISI was doing its best to hunt down the Taliban and al Qaeda. But the evidence suggested otherwise. In 2002, Musharraf's government arrested nearly 2,000 Islamist militants, including Taliban members. Within a few months, they were all released.

Musharraf was trying to be an ally both to America and to the Islamists who hated it, at the same time. "They're not sure we are staying [in Afghanistan]," one senior U.S. military commander told the *New York Times*. "And if we are gone, the Taliban is their next best option. [They're] hedging their bets."

in 1974, and Pakistan had raced to build its own bomb, succeeding in 1998. As part of the program, Khan built an international network to secretly obtain the necessary parts for uranium enrichment and weapons construction. In the eighties, he began selling some of those parts and the nuclear know-how to other nations, including Iran and North Korea.

After the U.S. revealed the network, Pakistan's military leader, President Pervez Musharraf, arrested Khan. But he quickly pardoned him and confined him to house arrest. Khan was a national hero, and most Pakistanis did not want him punished.

Khan's network and its discovery revealed a new frightening wrinkle on the issue of nuclear proliferation—as nations like Pakistan, Iran, and North Korea tried to develop nuclear weapons, they were all sharing information. The CIA had to try and figure out if other individuals like Khan were conducting black market nuclear deals with other nations or even terrorists.

## FINDING A COIN

The White House continued to be more focused on Iraq than Pakistan or Afghanistan. If American forces were ever going to be able to withdraw, an elected Iraqi government had to be able to control the country. Parliamentary elections were held at the end of the year. But the political process there was slow and messy. Iraq's ethnic and religious groups did not agree on much.

As for creating security for the Iraqi government, the U.S. military was learning some new lessons. A big one was the importance of counterinsurgency, known by its military nickname, COIN. Counterinsurgency recognizes that when facing an insurgency, killing the enemy is not the primary goal. The number one goal is to protect and help the civilian population. Doing that builds goodwill and dries up public support for insurgents, eventually causing the insurgency to wither and die. American commanders were realizing that their heavy-handed tactics in 2003 and 2004 had alienated the Iraqi population. Commanders began attending a special COIN school, where they learned the tactics for carrying out a successful counterinsurgency.

But the key part of COIN, providing security for the Iraqi population, was not getting easier. In 2004, there were 26,496 insurgent attacks on American troops. In 2005, there were 34,131. The insurgents were getting more sophisticated and attracting plenty of recruits. A U.S. Intelligence Community report on Iraq in January 2005 found that Iraq had replaced Afghanistan as the number one training ground for terrorists. Iraq may not have been part of the war on terror when Bush decided to invade in 2003, but it was now.

## STATE OF DENIAL

As the violence in Iraq worsened, anger against the war grew. But Bush kept insisting that things were going well. He had always been slow to admit problems or failures—he did not want to be seen as second-guessing his decisions. He felt confidence was important. But as the year went on, many Americans began to ask if the president was out of touch with events in Iraq.

Bush wasn't having much success domestically either. His big policy proposal, reforming Social Security, was dying a slow, painful death. The Social Security program provides monthly payments to retirees and the disabled. It's a safety net created by the administration of Democratic President Franklin Roosevelt during the Great Depression to protect financially vulnerable people like seniors from poverty. People pay Social Security taxes while they work and collect benefits when they retire.

But there was a financial problem facing Social Security. When members of the baby boom generation, those born in the decade after World War II, begin retiring around 2015, there will be more retirees than workers. Taxes paid by workers may not be enough to cover benefits for retirees.

Bush proposed a Republican solution—instead of simply paying Social Security taxes, workers could put most of the money that would have gone for Social Security taxes into investment accounts. The idea was that the money would grow with the stock market and each worker would have a nest egg once they retired.

Democrats opposed the idea. It would make citizens dependant on the stock market, which could be unreliable. What if you were set to retire and suddenly a recession began, wiping out the stock market and your retirement account? There was a spirited debate for months in Washington, but there was little public support for Bush's plan. What Bush had hoped would be a key part of his legacy failed miserably.

## WHEN THE LEVEES BREAK

Early on the morning of August 29, Hurricane Katrina made landfall in south-eastern Louisiana. The storm had crossed Florida days earlier and strengthened in the Gulf of Mexico, at one point becoming a Category 5 storm with sustained winds over 175 miles an hour. The Federal Emergency Management Agency (FEMA) and state and local governments had already been preparing and planning to help people after the storm, but there was a lot of confusion. In New Orleans, Mayor C. Ray Nagin did not issue an evacuation order until nineteen hours before the storm hit land. New Orleans was in a dangerous spot—built on low-lying land between the Mississippi River and Lake Ponchartrain. A strong enough storm could flood it entirely. A significant number of people in the city did not have cars or other ways to evacuate. New Orleans had always survived past hurricanes, so some people ignored the late order.

Katrina weakened as it came close to shore and hit the Mississippi coast head on. Communities along the Gulf of Mexico were devastated, whole towns destroyed. New Orleans appeared to escape a direct hit. While the storm was bad, the worst of it was to the east. But soon water began to flood parts of the city. The levees that ring New Orleans, which protect it from floodwaters from the river, lake, and many canals, and also facilitate shipping traffic, were failing in several areas and water was rushing in. Soon 80 percent of the city was flooded. People began climbing on their roofs, trying to stay above the water, which had mixed with garbage and sewage. Many, especially the elderly and the sick, became trapped in their attics and drowned.

The government response to both the storm and the levee failure was slow. While some agencies like the U.S. Coast Guard acted quickly and competently, others did not. FEMA seemed particularly unprepared to get to New Orleans, rescue people, and provide aid and shelter. State, local, and federal officials argued over who had control.

Meanwhile, the world watched in horror as television showed people trapped on their roofs, surrounded by water, in a major American city. Almost thirty thousand people had taken shelter from the storm in the Louisiana Superdome, an enclosed stadium downtown. They remained trapped there for days with no food, water, or electricity, waiting for help from the government of the richest nation on earth. Eventually the National Guard moved into the city, evacuated people, and restored order.

Bush once again appeared slow to grasp the problem. On vacation in Texas when Katrina struck, he flew over the

*Residents of New Orleans's Lower Ninth Ward wait for rescue boats. The city was spared a direct hit from Hurricane Katrina, but its protective levees failed.*

devastated area rather than touring it in person. A few days later, when he traveled to meet with state and federal officials in Mobile, Alabama, he told FEMA director Michael Brown, "Brownie, you're doing a heck of a job," when it was obvious FEMA was not. Bush eventually engaged more, but even in the months afterward, federal aid was slow. Hundreds of thousands of people wanted to return home and rebuild, but were slowed by lack of help and lack of money.

Along the Louisiana, Mississippi, Alabama, and Florida coasts, at least 1,836 people had died. There was over $85 billion in property damage. And Americans were unsure of their government. The Army Corps of Engineers had built the levees, but had put more money and manpower into keeping rivers open for commerce than into flood protection. Congress and local levee boards hadn't helped.

Some conservatives argued this was further proof that government bureaucracy was inherently incompetent. They also put most of the blame on Louisiana's Democratic governor. Some liberals put the blame squarely on Bush and argued it was proof that Republicans had gutted the government, rendering it ineffective. Most Americans just wanted to know that if they were victims of a natural disaster or terrorist attack, someone would help. At the end of 2005, it did not feel that way.

# 2006

## *You Have Six Billion Friend Requests*

IN 2006, ONE of the most popular TV shows in America was about a government agent fighting terrorism. Jack Bauer, the hero of *24*, frequently used torture while interrogating enemies for crucial information. While quail hunting in Texas, Vice President Cheney accidentally shot a friend in the face. (Thankfully the wounds were not serious.) On March 24, the Disney Channel debuted a new series, *Hannah Montana*, about a girl trying to be a normal teenager by day and a famous pop star by night. And the International Astronomical Union voted on an official definition of planet, demoting Pluto to a new category: "Dwarf Planet."

In 2006, seven explosions killed at least 186 people on crowded commuter trains and stations in the Indian city of Mumbai. Sudan rejected a United Nations resolution calling for a U.N. peacekeeping force in Darfur, saying this would compromise its sovereignty. British and Pakistani authorities broke up an alleged terrorist plot to simultaneously blow up as many as ten jets leaving Britain for the United States. New rules banned passengers from bringing liquids on board planes.

---

### WEB 2.0

In March of 2006, a Web developer named Jack Dorsey posted a short message on a new Internet service he and a few colleagues had devised: "just setting up my twttr."

Twitter would not be available to the

public for several months, but 2006 was the year that Web 2.0 and social media changed the Internet and the way people communicate.

The so-called Web 1.0, the early incarnation of the World Wide Web, allowed people to visit pages set up by someone else. People could read documents online, or buy things in a virtual store. Web 2.0 was about collaboration and community. Social media was people posting their own material—writing, music, video—online. In Web 1.0, people who knew enough code to make their own Web pages could post videos on their site for visitors to watch. The Web 2.0 version of this was YouTube, whose motto was "Broadcast Yourself." Created in 2005, the Web site allowed anyone to post videos for anyone to see, share, and comment on. (Google would buy it for $1.65 billion in November of 2006.) On MySpace or Facebook, people could put up their personal information, musings, or pictures and invite friends to visit. On blogs, people could comment, starting a conversation.

By February of 2006, more than a million people were registered on Wikipedia to write and edit entries.

These social media sites multiplied the Web's ability to spread ideas. Suddenly anyone could easily join a discussion. You didn't have to be a journalist or scholar to share information. Anyone who wanted to post their review of a new movie or restaurant or video game could do it online. A teenager in California could blog about her favorite novel. An Israeli teen could post a video diary on YouTube from a bomb shelter during Israel's 2006 war with Hezbollah on the Israel-Lebanon border. Everyone with Internet access had a voice.

And because anyone armed with a camcorder or a cell phone with a camera could now post what they saw on the Web, and anything shown once on TV could be put online, suddenly everything was available to the entire public. A video of Senator Conrad Burns of Montana falling asleep during a hearing, originally caught by C-SPAN, could be seen on demand on YouTube.

The video Web site's power became clear during the 2006 congressional elections. At a minor campaign event in southwest Virginia in August, Senator George Allen decided to mock S. R. Sidarth, a young volunteer from his opponent Jim Webb's campaign, who was videotaping all of Allen's events. He kept referring to Sidarth as "Macaca," a rarely heard word used by colonialists in Africa to refer to monkeys and native Africans. Sidarth was of Indian ancestry, but he had been born and raised in Virginia. Yet Allen pointed to him and said, "Let's give a welcome to Macaca, here. Welcome to America and the real world of Virginia." In the past, few reporters would have been at such an event and Allen's racist comment might never have been heard by most people. Instead, the video was viewed over and over, and Allen lost his reelection.

Of course, there were drawbacks to everyone having a voice. Comments on blogs showed that some people held racist or sexist views, and the Web gave them a public place to express them freely. Plenty of things posted were just silly or stupid. Small incidents were exaggerated by Web site contributors. Then there were blatant falsehoods. In May of 2005, journalist John Seigenthaler discovered an entry on Wikipedia claiming that he was a suspect in both the John F. Kennedy and Robert Kennedy assassinations. It wasn't true. Someone had edited the entry four months earlier as a joke.

But there were few safeguards to prevent such things, aside from other Web users catching and fixing such mistakes. Stephen Colbert coined the term Wikiality, a combination of Wikipedia and reality. In Wikiality, truth was based on consensus rather than fact—if a majority on the Internet agreed something was true, it was true. While Colbert was referring to Wikipedia, the term applied to all social media. These sites were more democratic, but their "truth" was determined by majority opinion, not facts or expertise.

## CIVIL WAR

In 2006, what had been an insurgency in Iraq became a civil war as Sunnis and Shi'ites began killing each other over who would control the country when the Americans left. The sectarian violence flared not long after elections were held at the end of 2005 for a parliament that would choose a prime minister to govern the country. Iraqis voted along sectarian lines—Shi'ites, Sunni Arabs, and Kurds each voted for their own ethnic groups. The Shi'ites had a solid majority, and for the first time in decades, Sunnis did not control Iraq.

The Sunni insurgents, who previously had mostly targeted Americans, turned on all Shi'ites. On February 22, a series of explosions destroyed much of the Al Askari Mosque in the city of Samarra. It was one of the holiest Shia sites in the world. The evidence suggested that an Iraqi offshoot

*U.S. soldiers secure a Baghdad street after a car bomb explosion, July 11, 2006. Three people were killed and seven wounded by the blast.*

of al Qaeda, led by a Jordanian named Abu Musab al Zarqawi, destroyed the mosque to ignite tensions between Shi'ites and Sunnis.

It worked. Shia militias and Sunni insurgents began terrorizing and killing civilians. In Baghdad, Shi'ites began an organized campaign to push Sunnis out of the city. Sometimes they would kill a few Sunnis in a certain neighborhood to send a message; other times they would kidnap or rob Sunnis. Sometimes they would merely send a letter with a bullet in it to a Sunni home. The message was clear—leave or die.

Sunni insurgents carried out similar terror campaigns in areas where there was a Shia minority. The U.N. reported that during the first six months of 2006, civilian deaths in Iraq increased by 77 percent, averaging about one hundred per day. They estimated that roughly fifty thousand Iraqi civilians had been killed in violence since the war began.

While the American media reported on the sectarian violence, for most Americans, who were understandably worried about U.S. soldiers, it was hard to imagine the terrifying daily lives of Iraqis. People were being dragged from their homes in the middle of the night and shot because of their religion. Kids trying to sleep at night could hear gunfire and mortar explosions. Bodies were found on the street every day. Hundreds of thousands of people decided that it was better to abandon most of their belongings and move to other countries rather than stay and face the violence.

There was hope that the new parliament and new Prime Minister, Nuri al-Maliki, would bring order when they took office in April. But Maliki did little—his support came from Shi'ites alone.

The Bush administration's plan for Iraq was for American troops to fight the insurgency and violence until the Iraqi army was trained and could take over. But it looked like the country would fall apart before that. Even when al Qaeda leader Zarqawi was killed by a U.S. bomb, the insurgency did not end. And when Saddam Hussein was executed by Iraqis for crimes against the Iraqi people, some of the guards could be heard chanting their support for Moqtada al-Sadr, a Shia militia leader. Even the dictator's death became a sectarian event.

## THE DECIDER

As the number of U.S. soldiers killed in Iraq rose to three thousand, many Americans asked whether the U.S. could succeed in Iraq. Bush appeared to be in denial. When critics called for Donald Rumsfeld to be fired over his handling of the war, Bush was dismissive. "I hear the voices, and I read the front page, and I know the speculation," he told reporters at the White House. "But I'm the decider, and I decide what is best. And what's best is for Don Rumsfeld to remain as the secretary of defense."

On the fifth anniversary of the September 11 attacks, Bush gave a speech emphasizing the link between succeeding in Iraq and winning the broader war on terrorism. "If we give up the fight in the streets of Baghdad, we will face the terrorists in the streets of our own cities." But a few weeks later, a classified National Intelligence Estimate leaked to the press concluded that the American presence in

*Donald Rumsfeld and President Bush attend a ceremony honoring Rumsfeld at the Pentagon, December 16, 2006.*

Iraq had actually had the opposite effect: "the Iraq war has made the overall terrorism problem worse." Iraq was becoming a valuable recruiting tool for al Qaeda and other Islamist terror groups.

Americans had reelected Bush in 2004 because they felt he was the best person to keep the country safe and to handle the war in Iraq and the war on terror. But polls showed they were changing their minds. When his second term started, he had an approval rating over 50 percent. By March 2006, one poll found it was at 33 percent. Even Republicans were starting to lose faith in him. The same March survey found that, "Until now, the most frequently offered word to describe the president was 'honest.' The single word most frequently associated with George W. Bush today is 'incompetent.'"

Iraq was the biggest issue troubling the president, but not the only one. On October 10, the North Koreans conducted a nuclear test explosion underground. It was a small blast—smaller than the bomb that the U.S. dropped on Hiroshima in World

War II. But it was enough for North Korea to declare itself a nuclear power. Bush's threats had done no good.

## RETURN OF THE TALIBAN

In the spring of 2006, as snow in the mountain passes between Afghanistan and Pakistan melted, hundreds of Taliban began streaming across the border into Afghanistan. They set up roadblocks, assassinated government officials, and burned schools. During the course of the year, there were 136 suicide bombings and 191 U.S. and NATO soldiers died. The Taliban were back.

Many of the Taliban and some al Qaeda members had been hiding in Pakistan's tribal areas for years, living in villages with Pakistani Pashtuns. They had found natural allies—there were several militant Islamist groups in the tribal areas. Allying with al Qaeda and the Taliban, these Pakistani militants gained money and training. They recruited sympathetic tribesmen to their cause. They began killing tribal elders, imposing harsh sharia law, and mounting attacks on Pakistani army forces. Soon these Pakistani militant groups would merge into one organization, Tehrik-i-Taliban Pakistan—the Student Movement of Pakistan.

The Pakistani army began sending more troops, trying to reassert control of the area. But they suffered humiliating defeats. The army was not trained to fight a counterinsurgency in the mountains. And the military campaign was politically unpopular. Most Pakistanis outside the tribal areas did not consider the Taliban a threat. They accused President Musharraf of fighting his own people because America ordered him to.

In September, Musharraf agreed to a ceasefire with the Pakistani Taliban. He removed his soldiers from the area and in return the tribes guaranteed that the Taliban would not attack Pakistani forces or cross over into Afghanistan to attack Americans. Of course, Pakistan had almost no border troops to monitor that promise. Worse, after the army withdrew, the Taliban began expanding their territory, taking over more villages.

## THE DARK SIDE COMES TO LIGHT

At home, Bush faced other problems. Many of the secret decisions he had made in the terrified climate after September 11 were now leaking out to the public. Five years after the attacks, some people began to claim that Bush had expanded presidential power too much.

For example, in late 2005, the *New York Times* reported that back in 2002, Bush had secretly authorized the National Security Agency to wiretap domestic phone calls and emails without obtaining legally required warrants. In August 2006, a federal judge in Detroit ruled the wiretapping program unconstitutional.

The administration was also being challenged for how it handled suspected terrorists. The media was finding out more details on the enhanced interrogation techniques Bush had approved. Human rights groups were issuing more vocal condemnations of the Bush policies, accusing the United States of engaging in torture.

Bush had decided back in 2001 that suspected al Qaeda members captured overseas would not be tried by U.S. courts. Eventually, he set up special military courts, or tribunals, to try them. Suspects were not given most of the rights defendants in U.S. courts had—the accused weren't allowed to see some of the evidence used against them; evidence possibly obtained through torture could be admitted; and the accused could not appeal to U.S. courts.

In June, the Supreme Court ruled that the military tribunals were unconstitutional because Bush had failed to obtain congressional approval. Moreover, the Court stated, the tribunals violated both the Uniform Code of Military Justice and the Geneva Conventions and omitted many of the safeguards of a proper trial. But Bush was able to convince Congress to pass a new law legalizing his rules for the trials. He also announced in September that he would close fourteen secret CIA prisons overseas and transfer all detainees to Guantanamo for trial.

While the new law legalizing the trials, the Detainee Treatment Act, allowed the tribunals to continue, it also set rules for how detainees could be interrogated. From now on, the military had to use interrogation methods from the Army Field Manual, a standard handbook. That meant enhanced interrogation techniques were not allowed. However, the law said nothing about what techniques the CIA could use. Critics alleged that the Bush administration still allowed torture.

## MIDTERMS

Congressional Republicans looked at the president's tanking approval ratings and were scared. Bush wasn't up for election in November, but Republican congressmen and many Republican senators were. As members of the president's party, they worried they would bear the voters' wrath against Bush.

They had other reasons to worry, too. Public opinion of the Republicans in Congress was sinking, and not just because of the president. The Republicans had been hit by several corruption scandals. In March former Republican congressman Randy Cunningham of California was sentenced to eight years in prison for taking at least $2.4 million in bribes from military contractors. Also in March, a powerful Republican lobbyist named Jack Abramoff was convicted of fraud, tax evasion, and conspiracy to bribe public officials. In June, powerful House majority leader Tom DeLay resigned from Congress because of an indictment involving improper fund-raising and the taint of his long association with Abramoff. In September, another GOP congressman was indicted for accepting tens of thousands of dollars' worth of bribes for helping Abramoff's clients.

Yet another ugly scandal engulfed Congress in October, when Florida Republican Mark Foley resigned from the House after it was revealed that for years he had been sending sexually explicit messages to teenage male congressional pages. The Republican leadership had known about the emails for months, but had done almost nothing about them.

Republicans had been in control of Congress since 1995, and had portrayed themselves as the party with strong moral values, strong policies on defense, and strong fiscal discipline. With the scandals, with Iraq growing worse by the day, and with the federal budget deficit swelling thanks to the cost of two wars combined with major tax cuts, the GOP now looked weak on all three points.

On November 7, the Democrats took advantage, winning thirty-one more seats in the House of Representatives and five seats in the Senate. They would be in control of both chambers. Bush now had to grapple with a Congress that opposed him on most issues. The day after the election, he fired Rumsfeld. The American people had decided.

## CHANGING THE WORLD A FEW DOLLARS AT A TIME

In a year of violence in Sudan, Iraq, Lebanon, Afghanistan, and numerous other places, many people learned for the first time about a man who was singlehandedly making the world a better place—and he didn't even have a blog. Muhammad Yunus was a symbol of self-empowerment.

He was known as the "banker to the poor." Born in Bangladesh and educated in the U.S., Yunus was an economics professor who wanted to prove he could make a difference in people's lives, so he began giving poor people in villages small loans to help them start businesses. These were people banks would not bother with—the loans were too small and the people too poor.

In 1974, Yunus had given a group of very poor women in the village of Jobra, Bangladesh, a loan of $27 out of his own pocket. The forty-two women wanted to make baskets and furniture by weaving bamboo, but lacked the money to start a business, and village loan sharks charged high interest rates. With Yunus's loan, their business was successful and they easily paid him back. Two years later, he founded the Grameen Bank to make small loans on a wider scale, mostly to people with no collateral who would not be served by typical banks. People called the idea "microcredit," and it spread to fifty-eight other countries. It gave thousands of people the opportunity to pull themselves out of poverty.

By 2006, Grameen had helped more than six million borrowers, the vast majority of them women. Late in the year, the Nobel committee awarded Yunus and his bank the Nobel Peace Prize, stating, "Lasting peace cannot be achieved unless large population groups find ways in which to break out of poverty." Yunus was not a Web 2.0 innovator, but he was proof that social networks and globalization could make a difference in people's live. It was possible to reach people all over the world, and, with a little investment, touch their lives.

# 2007

## *Double Down*

IN 2007, APPLE introduced the iPhone, which narrowed the gap between what you could do on your computer and what you could do on a cellular phone. The company sold more than 1.4 million iPhones that year. Track and field star Marion Jones relinquished five Olympic medals she won in the 2000 Sydney Games, after admitting to using performance-enhancing drugs.

In 2007, Nancy Pelosi became the first woman elected to be Speaker of the U.S. House of Representatives. Democrats took control of Congress, but failed to force President Bush to set a timeline for withdrawing troops from Iraq. A student at Virginia Tech killed thirty-two people including himself in a one-day rampage across campus. In Southeast Asia, the military dictatorship of Myanmar cracked down on peaceful democracy protests by thousands of Buddhist monks. The International Criminal Court issued arrest warrants against Sudanese accused of war crimes in Darfur.

---

### THE INCREDIBLE SHRINKING PRESIDENT

President Bush had hoped to remake America and the world when he began his second term. Now he appeared to have little power to remake anything. His approval rating continued to decline. Democrats took control of both chambers of Congress on January 4 and immediately began an ambitious agenda, passing bills increasing the minimum wage, reforming rules on contact between lobbyists and members of Congress, and expanding the State Children's Health Insurance Plan (SCHIP) by offering health insurance to ten million children who didn't have it. Bush vetoed some bills, including the SCHIP bill, but signed others into law.

Republicans in Congress were beginning to desert Bush. Some were frustrated and angry at White House policies—especially Bush's spending habits. Thanks to the tax cuts and two wars, the federal deficit had been rising dramatically. This upset fiscal conservatives. So when Bush looked to Republicans for help on his next major domestic policy initiative—immigration reform—he found little support and a lot of outright hostility.

Bush had been advocating for immigration reform for three years. In 2007, there were an estimated twelve million illegal immigrants in the United States. Many were Mexican, while others came from all over the world. Most wanted a better economic life than they had in their own countries, so they either sneaked across the U.S. border or obtained a short-term visa to enter America and did not leave when the visa expired. Because most had little money, they took tough jobs at the bottom of the workforce—such as cleaning houses, working in meatpacking plants, or sewing in clothing factories.

Immigration reform was a rare issue that cut across party lines. Some Democrats and Republicans believed that illegal immigrants were decent people trying to give their families a chance at a better life and the American dream, that the Mexicans crossing the border were no different from previous waves of immigrants from Ireland, Italy, Eastern Europe, or Asia. But other Democrats and Republicans argued that most of those previous immigrants had entered the country legally. Today's illegal immigrants had broken the law—allowing them to stay was unfair to those waiting to enter the country legally. They also argued that illegals took valuable jobs away from citizens. More extreme opponents of reform made intolerant and borderline racist arguments—that soon everyone in America would be speaking Spanish or that illegals wanted to make the U.S. a northern province of Mexico.

As a former governor of a state on the Mexico border, Bush was familiar with the immigration issue and he viewed illegals compassionately. And some of his political advisers saw the growing Hispanic population in the U.S. and believed the Republican Party should not alienate it. Bush's immigration plan proposed allowing some illegal immigrants to stay in the U.S. if they took certain steps to become lawful members of society. Bush argued that the illegals were not going away and it was better to integrate them into society than keep them on the margins. He also proposed measures to improve the legal immigration process.

Opponents of the idea argued that Bush was giving amnesty to people who had broken the law. And he might be encouraging more people to immigrate illegally. Most Republicans and some Democrats opposed Bush and defeated his efforts. Some also proposed their own bills, which would "get tough" on illegal immigration, putting up a seven-hundred-mile fence on the U.S.-Mexico border.

## SURGE

While Bush struggled with Congress over domestic issues, ironically, the one issue that had most eroded his support with the American people—the war in Iraq—was still largely under his control. Democrats tried to force Bush to set a timeline for withdrawal, but Bush vetoed their bill, and they did not override it. The Democrats had won the 2006 election by campaigning against the war. But they did not want to be accused of surrendering. While they tried to push Bush to change his war strategy, they did not take more aggressive action to force him to end it.

For four years, Bush and his staff appeared unable to admit that their strategy in Iraq was failing. When the insurgency began, they had insisted it was just a few Saddam loyalists who would soon be defeated. As things continued to worsen, they claimed it was not that the war was going badly, it was that the media wasn't reporting the good news from Iraq. Asked about Iraq just before the midterm elections, Bush had said, "Absolutely, we're winning."

But after losing control of Congress, the president began listening to other opinions. He fired Rumsfeld and appointed Robert Gates, a former director of the CIA who was known as a pragmatist, an innovator, and someone who, unlike Rumsfeld, knew how to manage people.

Gates asked his top commanders what they wanted. There were different opinions, but he ended up listening to several generals who had opposed the war in the first place. They argued that America needed to begin a comprehensive counter-insurgency strategy—provide security for the Iraqi people and help rebuild the country—and, eventually, support for the insurgency would dry up. And once the violence decreased, the Iraqi government could begin to assert real control over the country. While the commanders in Iraq had studied counterinsurgency, they had yet to introduce a comprehensive strategy. And without more troops, it was impossible to effectively provide security.

Skeptics argued against sending reinforcements. But Bush chose the so-called surge option, the deployment of more forces. On January 10, Bush announced that instead of beginning to withdraw troops from Iraq, he was sending 21,500 more. Eventually that number would rise to 30,000. And he approved Gates's decision to appoint General David Petraeus as the force commander in Iraq and Raymond Odierno as his top deputy. Both had argued for the surge. Petraeus was an expert in counterinsurgency—he had written the army's new manual on the topic, and he was an innovative thinker with a doctorate from Princeton in international relations. Odierno had also embraced the counterinsurgency strategy. Together, the two began to try and turn the war around.

The surge was risky. More troops meant more American lives in danger. The Iraqi government showed no signs of wanting to help end sectarian violence. If the surge failed, Bush would have few options left besides withdrawing in failure, leaving Iraq in chaos, and potentially destabilizing the entire region.

## A NEW NONPROLIFERATION STRATEGY

The change of course in Iraq was not Bush's only shift. Condi Rice, Bush's National Security Advisor in his first term and now secretary of state, was pushing for more engagement with the rest of the world. She wanted to put more emphasis on diplomacy and less on threats. It was a noticeable change in tone for the administration. Rice's biggest problem, however, was leverage. With the military bogged down and Bush's popularity so low, she had little influence with stubborn nations like Iran or even with potential allies like Russia and China.

North Korea's nuclear test in October

of 2006 seems to have convinced Bush that a new approach was needed. At the first National Security Council meeting after the test, Bush faced two choices—seek harsher sanctions from the U.N. Security Council or try talks with the North Koreans. Cheney continued to argue that talks would only reward the North Koreans for bad behavior. But diplomacy won the day. One person at the meeting said, "Cheney looked like he was going to be ill."

The State Department had talked with the North Koreans before, in multiple nation negotiations that included Russia, China, South Korea, and Japan. But White House officials had insisted that North Korea give up its nuclear program—its one bargaining chip—before the U.S. would agree to anything. Now the diplomats began more realistic negotiations, and in the summer of 2007, after the U.S. promised oil and other benefits, the North Koreans shut down the nuclear reactor at Yongbyon.

But the two nations were still far apart on North Korea's giving up its weapons fuel. As long as Kim's government had fuel and nuclear technology, his desperately poor nation could sell it. In fact, it had already sold nuclear expertise.

For six years, American spy satellites had been monitoring a building being constructed in eastern Syria in the middle of the desert. Analysts could not tell what it was. But in May of 2007, Israel's spy chief presented photos from inside the building to Stephen Hadley, Rice's replacement as National Security Advisor. The building was a nuclear reactor, a carbon copy of the Yongbyon reactor. The Israelis even had a photo of a top North Korean official visiting the site. Here, right next to Iraq, the North Koreans had been quietly selling their nuclear know-how. On September 6, Israeli jets flew into Syria late at night and bombed the unfinished reactor, destroying it. Soon Syrian bulldozers cleared the area, eliminating all evidence.

Rice's other proliferation concern was one of Syria's allies—Iran. But efforts to end Iran's uranium enrichment program had fallen apart in 2006 when Iranian President Mahmoud Ahmadinejad rejected negotiations. Bush asked the United Nations to enact economic sanctions against Iran, but Russia and China, both of whom had veto power on the U.N. Security Council, rejected the idea.

Rice worried that the Iranians would keep stalling on talks until they had enriched enough uranium for a bomb. Now she convinced Bush to allow her to offer one-on-one talks with Iran if the Iranians

## THE BEAR AND THE DRAGON

China's and Russia's resistance to tougher sanctions for Iran was part of a growing pattern. Both countries were enjoying economic booms. And both were taking stronger stands against U.S. policies, emboldened by their wealth and Bush's problems.

China's economy had been growing since the 1990s. The communist leadership had shifted from a communist economy to a limited capitalist one. The government still controlled much of the economy, but it allowed farmers and industrialists more freedom to build their own businesses. China enjoyed record growth throughout this decade.

China's government resented it when other governments lectured it on human rights. Thus it objected to international efforts to sanction other countries such as Iran. The Chinese had spent years building trade relations with countries the U.S. believed had poor human rights records—Sudan, North Korea, and Iran, to name a few.

Russia's economic boom was a comeback story. After the collapse of the Soviet Union in 1991, Russia had undergone a painful transition from communism to capitalism. Corruption was rampant and crime was widespread. And Russian pride was badly devastated as former territories such as Ukraine declared their independence.

When Vladimir Putin became president of Russia in 1999, he continued economic reforms but also exercised stronger control over certain industries (much as the Chinese did, but on a smaller scale). He worked to restore law and order. Critics complained that he did so by squashing democracy. But most Russians loved Putin's policies because he brought back national pride. And when oil prices rose dramatically from 2002 on, Russia, a leading oil producer, enjoyed an economic windfall.

There was talk that Russia was a major power again. Putin increasingly pushed against American policies in the world—as long as he believed America was interfering in "Russian spheres of influence" such as Ukraine, Russia would argue against American moves such as sanctions against Iran.

agreed to suspend enrichment. To her surprise, the Iranians refused. They would not stop enrichment even temporarily.

When Bush had invaded Iraq, he hoped it would send a message to Iran as well that he would not tolerate their nuclear program or their support for terrorism. The Iranians may have learned a lesson from the U.S. invasion, but not the lesson Bush intended. The U.S. had invaded a country that was only suspected of trying to build a nuclear weapon. It did not take the risk of invading North Korea, a country that already had them. The Iranian government may have decided that the only thing that would keep them safe from an American invasion was a nuclear weapon. By the end of 2007, the Iranians had more than 3,800 centrifuges spinning. If they spun uninterrupted for a year, they could make enough fuel for one bomb. The time to stop their race to go nuclear appeared to be running out.

## IS IT HOT IN HERE?

For decades, scientists had been finding evidence that carbon dioxide pollution was warming the earth, trapping heat from the sun that would normally dissipate into space. The evidence showed that the earth's atmosphere was getting hotter. Atmospheric levels of $CO_2$ were higher in 2005 than at any time in the past 650,000 years. Of the twelve warmest years on record, eleven occurred between 1995 and 2006. Most scientists and environmentalists worldwide wanted to take steps to reduce $CO_2$ pollution and hoped the U.S. government would lead the way, both by passing new regulations and by pushing for international agreements.

But many conservatives, including Bush, worried that rules against pollution would hamper businesses—raising costs for factories and for car manufacturers. They pointed out that a few scientists believed that it was not clear if $CO_2$ was to blame for rising temperatures, that average temperatures had fluctuated over earth's many centuries and this might be just a natural heat wave. And large segments of the public agreed. A 2009 poll by Pew Research Center found that, "While 84% of scientists say the earth is getting warmer because of human activity such as burning fossil fuels, just 49% of the public agrees."

Over its two terms, members of the Bush administration were repeatedly accused of ignoring recommendations from top scientists. In 2005, evidence emerged that a former chief of staff for the White House Council on Environmental Quality had personally edited documents summarizing government research on climate change before their release, weakening the documents' conclusions on climate change.

Former Vice President Al Gore visited Capitol Hill on March 21, 2007, to testify before Congress on climate change, and issued an uncompromising warning: "We do not have time to play around with this."

On April 2, 2007, the U.S. Supreme Court ruled that under the Clean Air Act, the Environmental Protection Agency had the authority to regulate greenhouse gases as a pollutant and was required to decide whether those gases were endangering human welfare. The Bush administration had argued that the EPA was powerless to pass such rules.

In response to the Supreme Court's decision, the administration dragged its feet. The EPA studied the issue again. In December of 2007, the head of the agency approved a report that declared that climate change imperiled the public welfare—a decision that would trigger national mandatory global-warming regulations—and emailed it to the White House. Top Bush aides, who opposed mandatory regulations, knew that if they opened the email attachment with the report, it would become public record, making it difficult to stop the regulations. So they didn't open it. They called the EPA chief and asked him to take back the draft. He did. And the following year, he issued a new version that did not call climate change a danger to public welfare. Bush took no action on the issue during his final years in office.

## SURGING FORWARD

As the surge strategy was implemented in Iraq, Generals Petraeus and Odierno had thirty thousand more troops, a new, energetic U.S. ambassador, and the faith of the White House. But that did not make their jobs any easier. Petraeus had been shocked when he arrived in Baghdad—vibrant Sunni neighborhoods he had walked in two years earlier were now ghost towns, abandoned because of sectarian violence between Shi'ites and Sunnis.

Petraeus quickly began making changes. U.S. troops became much more visible on the streets. Their new top priority was to protect Iraqi citizens. One intelligence officer noted that attacks on civilians were falling by autumn while attacks on Americans were rising. "If the attacks are against us, and not against Iraqi Security Forces or the people, we're winning."

In the heavily Sunni areas north and west of Baghdad, U.S. troops made a striking change—they began hiring some of the insurgents. This would not have been possible had local Sunni tribal leaders not tired of al Qaeda in Iraq. While al Qaeda's foot soldiers were local Iraqis, the leaders were foreign Islamists. In Iraq, a person's tribe has long been the most important bond. When al Qaeda leaders began bossing around tribesmen in the Western province of al Anbar and killing tribal sheikhs when their orders were ignored, a few tribes began rising up against them.

But the tribes were outgunned by al Qaeda, so they began approaching American units. Recognizing that most Sunni insurgents were fighting because they felt marginalized and under threat from the new Shia-led government, U.S. forces made a deal with the tribal sheikhs: The sheikhs could organize tribal militias to help the Americans protect Sunni towns, and the U.S. would provide funding and weapons. Young, unemployed men who might have been recruited by the insurgency were now recruited for the Sons of Iraq militias.

The political situation was still delicate—Prime Minister Nuri al-Maliki and his government were dragging their feet on stopping Shi'ite militias. They also did not like the idea of Sunni militias armed by the Americans. But the first signs of hope were emerging, and toward the end of 2007 violence began steadily decreasing.

## WE DO WHAT WE CAN

Testifying before Congress in the summer of 2007, Admiral Mike Mullen, chairman of the Joint Chiefs of Staff, said, "In Afghanistan we do what we can. In Iraq, we do what we must." Afghanistan remained an afterthought for much of the U.S. public. The military had far fewer troops there. Meanwhile, the Taliban were becoming increasingly aggressive in their attacks and controlled small enclaves across the country, especially in the south.

President Hamid Karzai was losing popular support. His government still could not provide security or aid to the people. Rebuilding continued to stall. There were not many economic opportunities for the people—one of the few was growing poppies, to make opium and heroin. In 2006 and 2007, opium production grew so quickly that Afghanistan became the source for 93 percent of the world's heroin. Some of the money from the drug trade went to the Taliban.

Across the border, in Pakistan's tribal areas, the situation was also deteriorating. The Pakistani Taliban were solidifying their control of the area, giving their fighters and al Qaeda a secure base from which to operate.

The Bush administration was worried about Pakistan for two important reasons. First, as long as the Pakistani government failed to eliminate the safe haven for al Qaeda and for the Afghan and Pakistani Taliban, it would be nearly impossible to win in Afghanistan. Second, the Pakistani Taliban were increasingly targeting the Pakistani government. If they took power, Pakistan's nuclear weapons would be in the hands of Islamist terrorists.

But the White House was still having trouble forcing the Pakistani government to take strong action against the Taliban. Pakistani President Pervez Musharraf was an unreliable partner. Plus, Musharraf was losing his grip on power. The Pakistani people were growing tired of his rule eight years after he seized power in a coup.

On November 3, faced with legal threats to his power by the Pakistani Supreme Court, which was questioning whether he could legally be president, Musharraf declared emergency rule, suspending civil liberties and firing the Court's chief justice. This provoked demonstrations across the nation. The Bush administration brought pressure on Musharraf to end the emergency rule and restore Pakistan's constitution. Musharraf eventually did.

Seeing Musharraf slowly losing control of the country but not wanting to abandon him and risk Islamists taking over, the Bush administration had been pushing the Pakistani leader to make some concessions in order to remain in power. Rice and her advisers negotiated a deal between Musharraf and the popular politician Benazir Bhutto, a former prime minister who was living in exhile after being forced out of office twice on corruption charges—charges that she alleged were trumped up by the military and rivals to get her out of office. Rice and the administration hoped Bhutto would win the upcoming election for prime minister. While her election would start moving Pakistan down the path back to democracy, Musharraf would keep firm control of the military and Pakistan's nuclear arsenal as president.

Musharraf allowed Bhutto to return

from exile. She quickly became the front-runner. She also became a target for Islamists, whom she opposed. "I think the time has come for democracy. If we want to save Pakistan, we have to have democracy," she said upon her return on October 18. "The terrorists are trying to take over my country and we have to stop them." But the Islamists were eager to stop her.

On the night she returned from exile, suicide bombers attacked her convoy. She was unharmed, but 136 of her supporters were killed. The Pakistani Taliban were growing more bold. On December 27, Bhutto was leaving a campaign rally when she was assassinated by members of the Taliban. The Islamists seemed to be threatening to take control of the country.

Bush would soon decide that he could no longer count on the Pakistani government to take action against al Qaeda and the Taliban, even as Pakistani Taliban militants were mounting daring attacks against that government. Six years after 9/11, with militants controlling the tribal areas and trying to infiltrate the rest of the country, 80 percent of the Pakistani military was stationed on the border with India. One top U.S. intelligence official visiting Pakistan was subjected to a long diatribe by a two-star Pakistani general that the problems in Afghanistan and the tribal areas were really a secret plot by India to weaken and conquer Pakistan.

For years, the U.S. had deployed Predator drones—unmanned planes—to hover miles above the tribal areas, looking for al Qaeda and Taliban members. They were not allowed to fire missiles at those militants without permission from the Pakistani government, however. A few months after Bhutto's death, when Bush realized he could no longer wait for a reliable ally in Pakistan, he stopped asking for permission and began authorizing more attacks.

## IOWA APPROACHES

There was an election approaching in America—the race for the White House. As 2007 drew to a close, the Iowa caucuses were just three days away. A crowded field of both Republicans and Democrats campaigned for the chance to succeed President Bush. It was a wide-open race—and the winner would determine the future of the country as it entered the next decade.

*Leading Pakistani Taliban member Hakimullah Mehsud (left) meets with Pakistani media in the tribal area of South Waziristan, October 4, 2009.*

# 2008

## *Change Has Come*

IN 2008, THE most talked about movie in America was *Slumdog Millionaire*, the story of a poor Muslim boy from an India slum searching for the love of his life. Among the best-selling novels was the Twilight series, a Mormon author's story of a teen girl in love with a vampire. At the Summer Olympics in Beijing, twenty-three-year-old Michael Phelps broke a thirty-six-year-old record by winning eight gold medals in swimming. And the world watched as China presented itself as a world power.

In 2008, Somali pirates terrorized international ships sailing in the Indian Ocean. The global economy fell into the worst crisis since the Great Depression of the thirties. Russia and its southern neighbor Georgia fought a war over South Ossetia, a Georgian province that declared independence. Pakistani Islamist terrorists killed 173 people in a series of coordinated attacks in India's financial capital, Mumbai. And Americans went to the polls to decide on a new Commander in Chief.

### THE AUDACITY OF HOPE

On January 1, Illinois Senator Barack Obama's campaign for president was in danger of being a disappointment. Obama had been a political phenomenon since he gained national attention for giving the keynote address at the 2004 Democratic National Convention when he was running for the Senate. But Obama had not wowed voters during the eleven months since he had announced his presidential candidacy. Some found him too intellectual, too cautious. Some found him boring.

It was perhaps inevitable that Obama failed to meet the incredibly high expectations Democratic voters had of him. To many, Obama seemed an ideal candidate based on his life history alone. As he put it, "in no other country on Earth is my story even possible."

Barack Hussein Obama was the only child of a white woman from Kansas and a black man from Kenya. His parents had met at the University of Hawaii. They divorced when he was a little boy, and Obama was raised by his mother, who remarried and lived in Indonesia for many years, and by his maternal grandparents, who lived in Hawaii. He met his father only a few times. Barack Obama senior died in a car crash when Obama was twenty.

After college, he spent three years in poor neighborhoods on Chicago's South Side as director of a community organization that helped poor residents with job training, college prep, and the defense of their rights. He then went to Harvard Law School, where he was the first African American ever elected president of the Harvard Law Review. After graduation, he returned to Chicago and served in the State Senate beginning in 1996. He won election to the U.S. Senate in 2004.

His unique biography, coupled with his appealing message, which called for an end to partisan divisions in America, made him a compelling symbol. And after two years in Washington, he decided he could do more for his country if he was president.

But he wasn't the only one who felt that way. With President Bush leaving office, the field was wide open in both parties. Nine Democrats and eleven Republicans jumped in. Polls showed that Americans wanted change, and every candidate in the race promised it.

Declaring your candidacy is one thing—raising the money to run a serious campaign is another. Donations are crucial in politics, and in the first three months of 2007, Obama and New York Senator Hillary Rodham Clinton each raised more than $20 million. It became obvious they were the main contenders for the Democratic nomination.

Clinton was considered the front-runner for several reasons. She had experience—she had been in the Senate for seven years and had played an active political role in her husband's administration. And most Democrats looked back on the Bill Clinton presidency with fond memories. Many women were electrified at the possibility of a female Commander in Chief. Clinton enjoyed a healthy lead in national polls throughout much of 2007. She stressed that these were dangerous times and she had the experience for the job.

Late in 2007, Obama started to be more aggressive. He went after Clinton's strength—her experience. Her time in Washington included years of partisan wrangling, and she had voted to give Bush authority to go to war against Iraq. "Dick Cheney and Don Rumsfeld had two of the longest résumés in Washington, but that experience didn't translate into good judgment," he noted during one debate.

The night before the Iowa caucuses, the first major contest in the fight for the nomination, polls showed a tight race. Obama had built a large operation of volunteers across the state and used the Web to organize them. But so had Howard Dean in 2004.

The Clinton campaign estimated that 90,000 Iowans would vote the next evening. Instead, 250,000 went to caucus—and more than 20 percent were under twenty-five years old. Obama won with 38 percent of the vote. Former vice presidential candidate John Edwards got 30 percent and Clinton came in a surprising third with 29 percent. Suddenly, Obama had momentum going into the New Hampshire primaries, just five days later.

But Clinton had suffered defeats before. She questioned whether Obama could deliver on his promises of hope and change. "Making change is not about what you believe; it's not about a speech you make. It's about working hard. I'm not just running on a promise for change. I'm running on thirty-five years of change. What we need is somebody who can deliver change. We don't need to be raising false hopes." It would be her theme during the primaries—Obama promised change, but she had the experience to deliver it. She won New Hampshire 39 percent to 36 percent.

In the next months, the results continued to seesaw. For the first time in sixteen years, the primary process did not produce an early clear winner. That suited Obama. He had built campaign organizations in almost every state. As the front-runner, Clinton had wanted to win big early. She had spent her resources in the early contests. Throughout February and March, Obama won primaries and caucuses in small states. But Clinton won big contests in places like Ohio and Texas. As the two continued to campaign, some

Clinton supporters accused Obama of sexism, while some Obama supporters accused Clinton of racism.

But a more serious racism charge arose when videos of Obama's Chicago pastor, Jeremiah Wright, surfaced showing him making controversial, sometimes racist comments in his sermons.

Obama had tried to avoid talking about race in the campaign, but the issue would have inevitably come up. If nominated, he would be the first black nominee of a major party. And while his biography was uniquely American, it was also different from that of many American politicians. Obama's middle name was Hussein and his father had Muslim relatives. Polls consistently showed that more than 10 percent of voters thought Obama was Muslim, no matter how often he made it clear that he was Christian.

On March 18, 2008, Obama gave a thirty-seven-minute speech condemning Wright's remarks, but also discussing race in America, including black anger over discrimination and white resentment over affirmative action and other civil rights programs. He said that while both feelings were rooted in legitimate grievances, they endangered America's ability to move into the future and solve problems together. Confronted with the race issue, Obama spoke in a way that reached out to all sides. The speech was watched 3.4 million times on YouTube in ten days.

It became obvious by the end of April that Obama would end the primaries with more delegates. On June 7, Clinton ended her campaign and endorsed Obama.

## REAGAN, NOT BUSH

The GOP primaries were also hard fought. Leading contenders included Arizona Senator John McCain, who had lost to Bush in the 2000 primaries, former Massachusetts Governor Mitt Romney, former Arkansas Governor Mike Huckabee, former Tennessee senator and actor Fred Thompson, and former New York Mayor Rudy Giuliani. As they stumped, raised money, and debated during 2007, none seemed an obvious choice.

Part of their challenge was overcoming voters' disapproval of President Bush. Throughout 2007, in various debates, all the candidates kept mentioning that they would continue Ronald Reagan's legacy—not George Bush's.

McCain might have been the favorite—he had done well in 2000 and was the only one who had run a presidential campaign before. But conservative Republicans did not trust him. While he had a conservative record, they believed McCain worked together with Democrats on bills too often and was not loyal. Radio host Rush Limbaugh claimed there was almost no difference between McCain and Hillary Clinton. McCain struggled to raise money throughout 2007.

At the first primary vote, in Iowa, the winner was a surprise—Huckabee, not considered a prime candidate, won 30 percent of the vote. An ordained Baptist minister, Huckabee was popular with social conservative voters.

In New Hampshire a few days later, the state's independent-minded voters backed McCain just as they had in 2000. Romney soon announced that he would drop out, but Huckabee refused. He continued to draw support from social conservatives who opposed McCain. But after McCain won Ohio and Texas on March 4, Huckabee announced he would withdraw.

## 8/8/8

While the U.S. was preparing for the presidential election, China was preparing for the Summer Olympics. Hosting the games in Beijing was a huge source of pride for the Chinese people, many of whom saw it as a sign that China was finally being recognized by the rest of the world as a great nation.

For centuries, China had been a great empire. But in the nineteenth century, the empire weakened, and European powers and America occupied parts of China and demanded special trade privileges. In the early twentieth century, Japan invaded and conquered much of China. After World War II, the country was divided by a civil war. The Chinese considered the nineteenth and early twentieth centuries a period a great humiliation.

By 2008, China had the second largest economy in the world (though it was still much smaller than America's economy) and was gaining influence on the international stage. But much of China's behavior in foreign policy was still shaped by its memory of the time of humiliation. Most Chinese wanted one thing from the rest of the world—respect. That meant recognition of China as a leading nation. It also meant not interfering in Chinese affairs. China was still a dictatorship—the Communist Party controlled the government. During the past two decades of economic reforms, the Party had effectively made an unspoken bargain with the people—leaders would deliver prosperity, liberalizing the economy enough to allow it to grow, and the people would not question the Party's political authority. Individuals who did faced arrest, imprisonment, even execution.

On May 12, a powerful earthquake ripped through mountainous Sichuan province in the heart of China. The damage was devastating. In one county, 80 percent of the buildings collapsed. Across the province, an estimated 69,181 people were dead, almost 19,000 were missing, and 5 million were suddenly homeless. Though the rescue and recovery process was difficult, China's government received praise from many for its rapid response.

But the praise quickly turned to criticism as Sichuan parents began protesting. An estimated 7,000 classrooms had collapsed in the province, killing, according to the official government report, 5,335 children. (Others estimate the number was as high as 10,000 children.) Many buildings around the schools survived the quake. Local officials had cut corners on school construction, using shoddy materials, sometimes keeping the budget money for themselves. The government censored any reporting on the scandal. Parents were given a cash settlement in return for agreeing not to protest. Some who continued to speak out were arrested.

By the eighth day of the eighth month of 2008, the focus was back on Beijing—the Olympics were beginning. (Eight is considered a lucky number in China.) The opening ceremony was an incredible show, created by Chinese film director Zhang Yimou. It used music and dance, along with plenty of special effects and fireworks, to highlight Chinese history and to show China as a tapestry of ethnic groups. One third of the world's population watched it on TV. China had arrived.

Many Americans saw China's new prosperity and grew concerned. Hearing about the 1.3 billion people of China, seeing the large amount of goods on U.S. store shelves made in China—from sneakers to computers—and seeing China taking an increasingly vocal role in world affairs, some wondered whether it would soon be challenging America as a superpower.

But as the collapsed schools in Sichuan made clear, China had plenty of problems. It was still a very poor country—among those 1.3 billion people, the average income was $1,700 in 2005, compared to $42,000 in the U.S. The government had been working hard to keep the economy growing at a record pace because that was the only way to create enough jobs for that many people. Still, 20 percent of the workforce had been unemployed in 2005.

## MAVERICK

John McCain secured the Republican nomination three months before Barack Obama claimed the Democratic nomination, but the head start did not help McCain. For most of the spring and summer, McCain struggled to find a message. His one successful line of attack was an ad that charged that Obama was more of a celebrity than a leader. He could give a good speech, Republicans alleged, but was all hot air, no substance.

Yet despite the McCain campaign's problems and the Republican Party's low approval rating, the two candidates were essentially tied in the polls at the end of the summer. Many pundits wondered why. Did voters feel they didn't know Obama well enough? Was it fear of someone different—someone black, with an odd name?

Hoping to get people to the polls in November, Obama's campaign worked hard to use modern technology to organize voters. That summer, the campaign decided to announce his vice presidential pick by text message. People had to register their cell phone numbers, allowing the campaign to collect voters' numbers and contact them during voter registration and get-out-the-vote efforts. The campaign gathered more than one million phone numbers.

The culmination of the effort came at the end of August, when Obama ended the final night of the Democratic convention by giving his acceptance speech not at the local basketball arena in front of only party members but at Denver's football stadium, in front of 100,000 people who lined up to see him. The price of admission? Attendees had to text friends and urge them to volunteer. Obama was joined on stage that night by his vice presidential pick, Senator Joe Biden of Delaware. The six-term senator had extensive foreign policy experience and working class roots, which Obama hoped would shore up some of his own weaknesses.

The next day, the McCain campaign stole some of Obama's post-convention thunder by surprising the world—McCain announced that Alaska Governor Sarah Palin would be his vice presidential pick. When an aide told Biden and Obama, Biden said, "Who's Palin?"

He was not the only person asking that question. Sarah Palin was in her first term as governor. Before that she had been mayor of Wasilla, Alaska, a suburb of Anchorage with about ten thousand residents. She had also held a state government position and questioned the ethics of some of her Republican colleagues, earning a reputation as a party rebel. McCain

*Republican presidential nominee John McCain and his running mate, Alaska Governor Sarah Palin, at a campaign rally, October 28, 2008.*

admired that. McCain also liked that Palin was an unusual pick. After meeting her just once, he signed her up. The media focused on Palin intently for weeks, trying to learn more about the newcomer. The scrutiny only intensified when it became known Palin's seventeen-year-old unmarried daughter, Bristol, was pregnant.

Conservatives loved Palin, who was not only very conservative on the issues but also spoke plainly, almost like George W. Bush. McCain began attracting larger crowds when she stumped with him. But after the initial buzz wore off, moderates and independents began questioning the selection. McCain had spent months saying Obama was too inexperienced. Now McCain, seventy-two and with a history of health problems, had picked a first-term governor of a state with less than 700,000 residents to be one step away from the presidency. Palin didn't help by looking ill-informed and nervous during several high-profile interviews.

As August ended, the media were all focused on Palin. But in September, economic news pushed the presidential campaign off the front pages. Wall Street, America, and the world were in serious financial trouble regardless of who became vice president in January.

## THE GREAT RECESSION

Owning a home is considered a cornerstone of the American dream—the government even offers tax breaks and other incentives to make it easier for people to buy a home. While there had been previous periods of great growth in the housing market, the real estate boom from 2000 to 2007 was unprecedented. Home values kept going up, so people kept selling their houses for a profit and buying larger ones, usually by taking out mortgages.

A mortgage is a loan from a bank that most people take out to buy a house. The buyer makes a down payment, the bank pays the rest of the home price, and the buyer pays back the mortgage plus interest over time. If a buyer can't pay the bank, he defaults and the bank sells the home to try and get its money back. If the homeowner sells the house before the loan is repaid, he pays off the remaining debt with the proceeds and keeps any money left over.

A homeowner can sometimes refinance a mortgage. Usually this is done if the home has escalated in value—the homeowner pays off the old mortgage by taking out a new one with better terms, such as lower interest rates or extra cash to pay for expenses like renovating the house.

Two things made this real estate boom

different from past ones. First, most banks had loosened the rules on whom they would lend to. Bankers decided that many people who had low incomes or bad credit and had been considered too risky for mortgages in the past were actually not that risky. The percentage of these borrowers who actually defaulted on their mortgages was very low. To encourage these potential borrowers, the banks created new types of mortgages to make it easier for them to afford a home. They offered lower down payments and mortgages with very low interest during the first two years, but very high interest after that. To avoid the higher interest rates, people would simply refinance. These new loans soon became very popular with homebuyers and very profitable for banks.

The second difference in this real estate boom was that Wall Street investment bankers found a way to make money off mortgages. Before, a bank would either hold on to a mortgage or, more often, sell it to another bank that specialized in collecting mortgage payments. It was profitable but not lucrative. Now, Wall Street banks discovered that they could create a new investment opportunity by buying a lot of mortgages, packaging them into a fund called a mortgage security, and then selling shares of the fund to investors. This proved far more profitable.

All of these new mortgages and mortgage securities were possible because Congress and the White House had been loosening regulations on the financial industry for decades. During the Great Depression, the government had created a lot of rules for banks and investors. But by the seventies, many of those rules were considered cumbersome and unnecessary. Both President Clinton and President Bush believed the rules should be relaxed, and Congress agreed.

As long as home prices kept rising and most people kept paying their mortgages on time, the mortgage lenders, the Wall Street bankers, and the investors all made money. Homeowners kept refinancing and using the money they borrowed to buy things like furniture, big-screen TVs, or SUVs. The banks assured people that mortgage securities were safe investments, but several experts argued that they were not. It was unrealistic to expect home prices to keep rising forever, and when they did fall, many Americans were going to be stuck with mortgages they could not afford. A writer in the *New Yorker* noted in 2002 that Americans had borrowed $350 billion since 2000 by refinancing their mortgages. What's more, they had already spent more than $100 billion of that on consumer goods. By 2006, Americans had borrowed and spent a lot more. An article in *Fortune* magazine noted, "The American home has become a virtual ATM."

Then, in late 2006, home prices began to fall. In many cases, owners' mortgages were bigger than what their homes were worth, and they couldn't refinance. People couldn't afford their payments. Throughout 2007 and 2008, more and more people began defaulting on their mortgages. Banks seized their homes. In some cases, the banks hired "movers" who showed up and started putting people's belongings on the front lawn.

Communities where the real estate boom had been the biggest—new suburbs that had sprung up during the good times in Florida, Nevada, California, and Arizona—were hit the hardest. People who were able to stay in their homes suddenly found themselves living in ghost towns. The houses around them were either empty after being seized by banks, or only half built, since it no longer made sense for construction companies to finish them. As home values sank, people's wealth shrank, so even those who kept their houses stopped spending as much. That hurt businesses, which started laying off workers, making the problem worse.

The real estate bust was bad, and by the end of 2007, the economy had slowed into a recession. But Wall Street's hunger for mortgage securities turned the recession into a global financial crisis. When homeowners began defaulting on their mortgages, investors began losing all the money they had put into mortgage securities. Suddenly people realized how risky these investments were. Panic began to build in the stock markets. Over the next few months, some of Wall Street's oldest, most important banks went bankrupt or were bought by other banks.

The country had not faced a financial crisis so dire since the Great Depression, almost eighty years earlier. During the start of the Depression, when Wall Street panicked, many of the biggest banks had failed. The federal government had done little to stop the carnage. People with money in the banks lost it all. This time, the government was more aggressive, led by the secretary of the treasury and the chairman of the Federal Reserve Bank, the central bank of the U.S., which supervises all other banks and works to keep the economy stable.

Secretary of the Treasury Henry Paulson, a former investment banker, and Ben Bernanke, the chairman of the Federal Reserve and an expert on the Great Depression, tried several different approaches to solve the crisis. They let some banks go bankrupt. They helped healthy banks buy troubled banks. And they sometimes invested taxpayers' money to keep banks afloat. By September it looked like every investment bank on Wall Street was in trouble, the stock markets were in a free fall, and the damage was spreading to banks in other countries. So Paulson and Bernanke went to Congress and asked for $700 billion to buy bad mortgage securities from the banks, clearing their balance sheets of these risky investments. Members of Congress were reluctant. Why should American taxpayers bail out Wall Street bankers who had made millions of dollars each year?

Though Wall Street seems far removed from most people, the truth is that all Americans have a stake in the stock market. Many invest through their 401(k) retirement plans. And businesses all across the country, from small stores to family farms, cannot operate and expand if they can't borrow money from their banks. After the big banks failed, companies all over the country would face bankruptcy and millions of people might lose their jobs.

## COOL HEADS PREVAIL

McCain was at a rally in Florida on the day in September when the worst of the crisis hit the stock markets. Despite the obvious peril the economy faced, he told the crowd, "The fundamentals of our economy are strong." In Colorado on the same day, Obama said, "It's not that I think John McCain doesn't care what's going on in the lives of most Americans. I just think he doesn't know. Why else would he say, today, of all days, just a few hours ago, that the fundamentals of our economy are strong? Senator, what economy are you talking about?"

Economic issues were not McCain's strength, and he proved that over the next few days, making several more odd statements, appearing to have no clear ideas on how he would help the economy if he were president. When the $700 billion bailout plan was proposed, McCain suspended his campaign, postponed a debate with Obama scheduled for two days later, and headed to Washington to help negotiate the bailout bill. McCain thought his move showed bold leadership.

But his role in the negotiations went poorly. Many Republicans and Democrats were opposed to the bailout plan—they knew most voters did not want them to rescue Wall Street, no matter what the long-term consequences were. The bill was defeated in a vote by the House, and McCain looked powerless as he tried and failed to convince his own party to back the plan.

Congress did pass the bailout eventually, but only when the stock market took another nosedive after the bill's defeat. And McCain did show up for the first presidential debate. Many in the press called his campaign suspension a stunt.

McCain did not realize it, but he was undoing the effect of his biggest strength—his experience. His campaign was erratic and undisciplined. Obama, on the other hand, looked presidential—he urged people to stay calm, proposed ideas for what he would do as president to help the economy, but stayed out of congressional negotiations where he thought he would be a distraction. His maturity was what many undecided voters wanted in a president at a time when the economy was in a free fall and the country seemed to be trapped in two wars.

As McCain began sinking in the polls and an Obama victory looked probable, anti-Obama rhetoric began to emerge from right-wing McCain supporters claiming that Obama was secretly a Muslim terrorist. "I am just so fearful that this is not a man who sees America the way you and I see America," Palin said at one event. At another, McCain worked hard to correct a woman who claimed Obama was "an Arab." (In the heat of the second presidential campaign since 9/11, sadly, no one spoke out to say there is nothing inherently wrong with being a Muslim, an Arab, or an Arab-American.) It was obvious that even if Obama did win the election, there were some voters who would not accept him as their leader.

## CHANGE

On Tuesday, November 4, 63 percent of eligible voters showed up at the polls, the highest percentage since 1960. All those enthusiastic voters helped swing several usually Republican states to Obama, including North Carolina, Virginia, and Indiana. By nighttime, it was clear the Illinois senator would win. He ended up receiving 52.9 percent of the popular vote to McCain's 45.7 percent. And he won 365 electoral votes, taking twenty-eight states, Washington, D.C., and one congressional district in Nebraska.

At midnight, Obama went before a sea of supporters in Chicago's Grant Park to make his victory speech. He began, "It has been a long time coming, but tonight, because of what we did on this day, in this election, at this defining moment, change has come to America."

*Barack Obama and his daughter Sasha celebrate his victory onstage during an election night gathering in Chicago's Grant Park, November 4, 2008.*

# 2009

## *Is Compromise a Dirty Word?*

IN 2009, AMERICA inaugurated a new president. Barack Obama, his wife, Michelle, and their two young daughters moved to 1600 Pennsylvania Avenue, adopted a dog named Bo, and planted a vegetable garden on the White House lawn. The Beatles were reunited in a video game, the latest edition of Rock Band. Sarah Palin resigned as governor of Alaska and went on a book tour to promote her autobiography. Pop star Michael Jackson died at age fifty of a heart attack.

In 2009, the global economy confronted the worst recession of modern times. In America, unemployment exceeded 10 percent. An outbreak of a new strain of flu, H1N1, quickly became a pandemic. Israel invaded the Gaza Strip for twenty days in an effort to stop Hamas from launching rockets into southern Israel. The International Criminal Court issued an arrest warrant for Sudanese President Omar Hassan al-Bashir for crimes against humanity in Darfur. Iranian protesters used Twitter to document demonstrations against their government.

---

### PERIL AND POSSIBILITY

As the day of his inauguration approached, Barack Obama may have asked himself—Why do I want this job? But as he told PBS shortly after he took office, "I think that we are at an extraordinary moment that is full of peril, but full of possibility. And I think that's the time you want to be president."

The two months between Election Day

and the inauguration are normally when presidents-elect focus on hiring staff and planning how to implement an agenda once they take the oath of office. But as Obama met with his various advisers on the problems the country faced, he realized he did not have time to wait. President Bush was a lame duck with little political influence. The economy needed help now.

So Obama began speaking to the country about how he was going to tackle the crisis. He and his economic advisers began drawing up a strategy to stop the bleeding and stimulate the economy. By the time he left Chicago for Washington, plans were already being executed.

Obama also was already facing the threat of terrorism. Credible intelligence surfaced in the days before his inauguration that a group of Somali Islamists might try to detonate a bomb somewhere on the Washington Mall during his swearing-in. The intelligence eventually proved a false alarm, but it was obvious that a new president did not mean an end to the threat of terrorism.

On January 20, Obama stood on the steps of a capitol building constructed by African slaves, put his hand on a Bible last used by Abraham Lincoln, and took the oath of office as the forty-fourth president, while a record-sized crowd watched. In his inaugural address, he acknowledged the challenges the nation faced: "Now, there are some who question the scale of our ambitions, who suggest that our system cannot tolerate too many big plans. Their memories are short, for they have forgotten what this country has already done, what free men and women can achieve when imagination is joined to common purpose, and necessity to courage. What the cynics fail to understand is that the ground has shifted beneath them, that the stale political arguments that have consumed us for so long no longer apply."

There was an incredible sense of history that day, as many traveled to the capital to see the nation's first African American president sworn in. But Obama did not have time to focus on that. "Obviously, at the inauguration, there was justifiable pride on the part of the country that we had taken a step to move us beyond some of the searing legacies of racial discrimination in this country," he later said. "But that lasted about a day."

He quickly took several symbolic steps. On January 22, he signed executive orders banning torture in interrogations and pledged to close the prison at Guantanamo Bay in one year. That meant prisoners would have to be released, handed over to other governments, or brought to the U.S. for trial by either federal courts or military tribunals. Ten months later, the Justice Department announced that 9/11 mastermind Khalid Sheikh Mohammed and four accomplices would be tried in a federal court in New York. Obama wanted to prove that the U.S. would remain faithful to its own laws. Critics accused him of endangering America by not being tough enough on terrorists. By the end of the year, a trial outside New York was being considered.

Obama also signed an order asking the Transportation Department to develop higher fuel efficiency standards for cars. And on his first Saturday in office, when he released a weekly radio address, as presidents have done since Franklin Roosevelt's time, Obama also released the address on a video posted on YouTube. He would post a new video every week.

## STIMULATING THE ECONOMY

But it was the economy that dominated his first hundred days in office. The Federal Reserve was already loaning money to banks to convince them to begin lending again. The administration also developed a plan to help some homeowners renegotiate the terms of their mortgages so they could, hopefully, remain in their homes.

To get the economy moving, the administration wanted to pass a stimulus package. Most economists backed the idea, arguing that when businesses stopped spending money, the government should step in and spend money on various projects instead, helping create jobs. In September, there had been talk of a $150 billion package. By January, economists were calling for between $500 billion to $1 trillion to be spent. A bill was introduced in the House of Representatives on January 25.

Obama started meeting regularly with congressional members from both parties, trying to develop bipartisan support for the stimulus bill. He hoped that his victory and the desperate state of the economy would influence moderate Republicans to work with him as long as he listened to their concerns. But most Republicans had a different view of what the stimulus bill should be. They wanted a small package—$500 billion or less—that consisted mainly of tax breaks for businesses. They argued this would encourage companies to start spending money again. Democrats wanted federal spending on unemployment benefits and money to create new jobs in education, health care, and infrastructure such as roads, bridges, and more environmentally friendly buildings. If the government invested in these industries, they argued, the economy would begin growing and then businesses would start spending.

It became clear that most Republican congressmen did not want to work with the president. And their most loyal supporters, according to polls, did not want them to compromise. When the House voted on the stimulus bill, not a single Republican voted for it.

While Democrats had a sizable majority in the House, in the Senate, Obama had to attract some Republican votes. He also had to lock down the support of several moderate Democrats who thought the bill's $900 billion price tag was too large. Obama urged voters to lobby their senators to pass the bill. Meanwhile, his staff negotiated until they crafted a bill that won the support of every Democratic senator and three Republicans. The final cost was $787 billion.

## A FOUNDATION

Obama learned something from the stimulus battle: Congressional Republicans had decided their best strategy for recovering from their election losses in 2008 was simply not to compromise with the president's agenda. So when the White House began lobbying for its budget proposal, it did not focus on Republicans. Instead, the president stumped for it by visiting key states as if he were a candidate again.

His budget was ambitious—a $3.5 trillion proposal that included funding for health care reform and new investments in education and energy technology. Critics called it too much. With the economy in trouble and two wars already costing trillions of dollars, shouldn't the president cut back on his agenda?

Obama countered that this crisis was not a time to delay addressing big problems—it was the perfect time to tackle them. On April 14, he gave an address laying out his strategy. He mentioned a Bible passage that compares two men, one who built his house on a foundation of sand, and the other who built his house on a foundation of rock. America, he warned, had built its house on sand—by relying so much on the financial industry while weakening the rules that regulated it, by relying on oil and coal for energy despite the environmental costs, by building a health care system that was among the most expensive in the world but did not provide the most effective care, and by having a political system where people focus on the short term—lurching from one crisis to the next without addressing fundamental problems. He said he hoped to help the country start building on rock.

Congress passed his budget. And polls showed that the president had America's approval. Back in October 2008, one poll had shown that just 8 percent of Americans believed the country was heading in the right direction. By April 2009, the same poll showed 51 percent believed it.

## A NEW BEGINNING

On June 4, Obama gave a speech at Cairo University in Egypt titled "A New Beginning." It was an effort to reach out to the Muslim world. He acknowledged Muslim contributions to both the world and America, and he spoke about the Israeli-Palestinian conflict, terrorism, and Iran's nuclear program. He also acknowledged past American interference in the region. On Iraq, he said, "Although I believe that the Iraqi people are ultimately better off without the tyranny of Saddam Hussein, I also believe that events in Iraq have reminded America of the need to use diplomacy and build international consensus to resolve our problems whenever possible."

The speech was well received. But some said that talk was cheap—they wanted Obama to prove his new diplomatic approach through action. Building a new foreign policy was not going to be a simple matter of nice words.

When it came to Iraq, America's involvement was winding down. Obama had announced in February that most of the 142,000 U.S. troops there would leave in August 2010. Roughly 35,000 to 50,000 would remain to train and advise Iraqi security forces and hunt terrorist cells until the summer of 2011.

## MAHMOUD II

Another part of Obama's foreign policy was his attempt to improve negotiations with Iran. He was willing to hold direct talks among Iran, the U.S., and America's allies. But he made it clear that if Iran continued its secretive nuclear enrichment program, there would be consequences, including economic sanctions. He also made several gestures toward the Iranian people, trying to move past the thirty years of hostility between the two nations.

Little would be accomplished before Iran's presidential election in June, though. Mahmoud Ahmadinejad was running for reelection against three challengers. The strongest was former prime minister Mir Hossein Mousavi.

Ahmadinejad had supporters, but many Iranians were angry with him over the poor state of the economy. In past elections, high turnout favored reformist candidates, and turnout was very high on that election day. So Mousavi supporters were shocked when the Interior ministry quickly announced the results, saying that Ahmadinejad had won in a landslide with 63 percent of the vote, compared to 34 percent for Mousavi.

Several analysts who looked at the results claimed they were fraudulent. While they believed the race was close enough that Ahmadinejad might have won, his margin of victory was suspiciously high. Ahmadinejad had traditionally done well in rural areas and poorly in big cities, but this time he received equally high margins in both. He even won a majority in Mousavi's hometown.

The next day, Mousavi supporters began protesting in cities around the country. For the most part, they were peaceful. But the government was not in the mood for challenges. The police began arresting reformist leaders. The Basij militia—part of the Revolutionary Guards, a special, elite branch of the military—showed up at rallies dressed as civilians and began beating protesters. When Neda Agha-Soltan, a young woman who supported reform, was shot at a rally on June 20, her death was caught on video and posted on YouTube and Facebook, sparking international outcry.

The protesters used Web sites like Facebook and Twitter to communicate and organize. The Iranian government responded by blocking the sites, jamming Western TV broadcasts, and interfering with cell phone service to stop text messaging. But the arrests were even more effective. Soon, hundreds of people were locked up. Some were beaten and forced to "confess" that the protests had been the idea of Great Britain and the United States. Protesters bravely continued their rallies for several more weeks, but the government would not back down and was soon putting reformists on trial. Some faced execution if convicted.

Obama was stuck negotiating with Ahmadinejad's government on Iran's nuclear program. But he had new proof of Iran's deception, evidence that might sway the international community to take stronger action. At some point in recent years, U.S. intelligence had discovered a second, secret uranium enrichment plant on a Revolutionary Guard base outside the city of

Qum. It looked highly suspicious—a small plant, too small to create much fuel for a nuclear reactor, but perfectly capable of producing enough fuel for a weapon.

Iran realized in September that the U.S. had discovered the facility. Ahmadinejad's government suddenly declared its existence to the IAEA. The U.S. responded by presenting the agency with evidence that Iran had hidden this plant from the world since 2002. With this new intelligence, Obama rallied support from Britain, France, Russia, and, to some extent, China for stronger sanctions if the Iranians failed to negotiate an agreement that would convince the world it was not producing nuclear weapons. At the end of the year, Iran was stalling, trying to drag out negotiations.

## NO CHANGE

As the political battles between the new president and Republicans continued, anti-Obama voters became increasingly vocal. To a certain degree, they were tapping into anger felt by many Americans. On March 16, it was announced that American International Group (AIG), an insurance giant that had received $170 billion in government funding to avoid collapse, would pay $165 million in bonuses to its executives. For the millions of Americans who were unemployed or struggling to keep their homes, the idea that Wall Street bankers who received government aid would now pocket million-dollar bonuses was appalling. AIG was not the only offender. Other Wall Street firms that had accepted government help paid bonuses. The firms claimed that if they didn't give bonuses, their most talented staff members would leave.

While the Bush administration had initially bailed out AIG, Obama had intervened to save General Motors. The auto manufacturer was in danger of bankruptcy, and because so many jobs depended on the company, the administration had stepped in and used taxpayer money to buy GM. The hope was that after restructuring, GM would once again be profitable and the government could sell it. The plan was unpopular with many Americans, who argued that GM had failed to innovate enough to make money, so it should be allowed to fail.

But the most virulent Obama opponents were angry about a lot more. They claimed that Obama had a secret "socialist" agenda; that the government aid to banks and General Motors were really industry takeover attempts. (These allegations ignored the fact that President Bush had begun the aid programs.) Some even claimed that Obama had not been born in the United States and thus was not a "legitimate" president. And when Obama proposed health care reform, his opponents declared that he wanted the government to control the health care industry, that he would have bureaucrats decide who got medical care.

Health care reform was Obama's biggest domestic priority. It was a politically sensitive issue no one had been willing to tackle head on since President Clinton's reform plan had failed more than fifteen years earlier. Obama argued that the U.S. health care system needed reform because it cost way too much and left too many people without insurance. The health care industry accounted for one out of every six dollars America spent. If costs were not cut, health care would bankrupt the country in the next few decades. The system was the most expensive in the world. Yet medical statistics showed that Americans were not receiving the best care possible. Moreover, millions of people had no health insurance at all.

Obama set key priorities for Congress. He wanted a health care bill that provided almost everyone with health insurance; that increased efficiency—by using proven techniques, eliminating unnecessary tests, and sharing data electronically—and prevented insurance companies from denying coverage to customers.

The White House expected a lot of give-and-take as lawmakers hashed out the details of the plan. They did not expect angry opponents who claimed the plan would empower the government to execute old people. During the summer, as lawmakers held town hall meetings in their home states and districts, protesters disrupted the meetings, shouting down the congressmen or senators and making all kinds of dire—and false—claims about the bill, alleging that it was a secret government takeover of health insurance or that government "death panels" would decide if seniors could keep receiving medical care or would be abandoned to die.

People had legitimate disagreements over what the bill should contain. Many conservatives felt the government should impose fewer rules on insurance companies. Some liberals believed Obama's plan did not go far enough. But it was hard for the nation to have a discussion when protesters marching on Capitol Hill compared Obama to Adolf Hitler and health care reform to the Holocaust. When Obama tried to explain the plan in a special joint session of Congress, South Carolina Congressman Joe Wilson yelled, "You lie!" in the middle of the speech, an unprecedented interruption. Wilson apologized privately, but was soon receiving millions of dollars in campaign donations from Republican voters.

By the end of 2009, the House and Senate had passed bills, but negotiations were still under way for a final bill the president could sign.

And it was clear that each of Obama's major proposals was going to require a full-on partisan battle. As the end of the year arrived, the president's approval ratings were dropping. Some of that was due to the poor state of the economy. The recession had officially ended, but jobs had not reappeared. People were beginning to ask why his measures hadn't fixed things yet. Others wondered if it was impossible for government to get things done.

But part of the decline in Obama's approval rating was due to a powerful anti-establishment feeling in the country. Polls showed most Americans believed the country was not in a good place and that life might not be better for their children. After a decade bookended by terrorism and financial catastrophe, people began to accuse business leaders and politicians—all politicians—of failing the country.

## AFPAK

On the night of August 5, Baitullah Mehsud went up on the roof of his father-in-law's house in South Waziristan, one of Pakistan's western tribal regions. Mehsud was a top leader in the Pakistani Taliban and was blamed for the assassination of Benazir Bhutto and several other major attacks. While he lay on the roof, an unmanned drone was flying two miles above, piloted remotely by a CIA staffer who was watching Mehsud on the drone's camera. The drone fired a missile at the house, and Mehsud was killed.

Eight years after 9/11, America was still fighting al Qaeda and its allies in Afghanistan and Pakistan—which the administration referred to as AfPak, noting the cross-border nature of the problem—and still trying to figure out its alliance with the Pakistani government. The drone strikes had been one of its most effective weapons.

For years, the Pakistani army had been content to allow the Pakistani Taliban to control the tribal areas. Many Pakistanis were convinced that the militants were harmless and America was exaggerating any threat in order to weaken Pakistan. But beginning in 2007, the militants began attacking targets in the rest of the country, and early in 2009 they took control of an area called the Swat Valley, not far from the capital of Islamabad. They imposed their strict version of sharia law. Pakistanis were horrified when a video surfaced of a seventeen-year-old girl being publicly flogged for not marrying a man her brother had selected.

The Pakistani army drove the Taliban out of Swat. Next they began a campaign in the tribal areas. The Taliban responded with terror attacks on major targets, including army headquarters and ISI headquarters. It's clear that the militants would like to overthrow Pakistan's government and take control of the country's nuclear arsenal. Pervez Musharraf resigned in 2008, and Bhutto's widower, Asif Ali Zardari was elected president, but the government was still unstable at the end of 2009.

Across the border in Afghanistan, the government was even less stable. On August 20, Hamid Karzai appeared to win a second full term as president. But evidence soon surfaced that his officials had stuffed the ballot boxes. He eventually agreed to a runoff, but his opponent withdrew, arguing there was no guarantee Karzai wouldn't cheat again.

America had high hopes for Karzai when he first emerged as a leader in 2001. But Afghanistan's challenges appear to have been too much for him. He had pushed the country's various corrupt warlords out of his government in 2005, but without their help, he had little actual control over the country. He realigned with them for the 2009 election. Many of the governors and local officials he appointed were corrupt. His own brother was reportedly both taking money from the CIA and helping the heroin trade in Kandahar province. Meanwhile, the Taliban were taking over small pockets all around the country, appointing their own governments, and punishing anyone who had worked with the Americans.

Obama was frustrated by Karzai's ineptness. He needed a strong ally in the Afghan government because he hoped to pursue a more aggressive strategy to push the Taliban out. Obama deployed 17,000 more U.S soldiers to Afghanistan at the start of his term. And that was just the beginning. To pursue a counterinsurgency strategy similar to the surge in Iraq, U.S. General Stanley McChrystal wanted 40,000 more troops to assert control and bring stability to most Afghan towns and cities. The additional soldiers would also allow the U.S. to train an Afghan army.

After a lengthy debate, Obama decided to send 30,000 more troops, hoping that would bring stability to enough of the country and accelerate the training of an Afghan army. But he also pledged to begin bringing troops home in the summer of 2011. He did not say how long that with-

*U.S. Marines meet with Afghan elders in the village of Mian Poshteh, Afghanistan, July 5, 2009. The marines helped push Taliban forces out of the area, and were working to provide security and aid to the locals.*

drawal would take, however. Afghanistan and Pakistan will likely remain an issue for America for years to come.

And they are not the only countries al Qaeda operates in. That was made clear on Christmas day, when a Nigerian Islamist tried to blow up a plane flying from Amsterdam to Detroit with explosives sewn into his clothes. The man had trained with a branch of al Qaeda in Yemen, a war-torn country south of Saudi Arabia. Al Qaeda is also suspected of building new training camps in Somalia and continuing to recruit potential terrorists in countries around the world, including the U.S.

Obama understood the price of his December decision to send more troops to Afghanistan. Three months earlier, he presided over a moment of silence for the victims of 9/11 on the eighth anniversary of the attacks. Five weeks after that, late at night, he visited Dover Air Force Base in Delaware. A military plane landed, carrying the bodies of eighteen soldiers killed in Afghanistan. Obama met with their families, and then watched and saluted as the coffins were unloaded.

# EPILOGUE

## *The Next Ten-Year Century*

AS A NEW decade approached, people gathered in Times Square once again to celebrate. Would the next ten years be just as frenetic as the last ten?

Across America, the attitude was far less optimistic than in 1999. *Time* magazine's Web site asked if the past decade was the worst ever. A *New York Times* columnist called it "the big zero"—"From an economic point of view, it was a decade in which nothing good happened, and none of the optimistic things we were supposed to believe turned out to be true."

Perhaps the pessimism is unavoidable when the unemployment rate stands at 10 percent. But at the same time, even the pessimists might be forgetting far darker times in history. And in today's Twitter and blog-driven society, they may also be acting a tad overdramatically.

All the same hopes and fears that people felt in 1999 are still alive today. But the current bad times may have focused Americans more on the fears and less on the hopes. Technology continues to bring the world closer together. At the same time, it makes it easier for extremists to launch horrible attacks. And our constant flow of information from the media makes every crisis seem all the more dramatic. Globalization has brought wealth to many corners of the world. But it also allowed financial problems in one country to trigger a severe recession across the globe. And as both the earth's population and the quest for prosperity grow in coming years, people will be competing more and more for precious resources like clean water and food. Climate change will only exacerbate these issues.

There are certainly unforeseen breakthroughs hidden in the years that lie ahead. There are also unforeseen problems. But the best prescription for solving the problems and taking full advantage of the breakthroughs lies in learning about the world and always trying to understand the times we live in.

# SOURCE NOTES

## **INTRODUCTION:** MAY YOU LIVE IN INTERESTING TIMES

"The Age of . . .": Ramo, *The Age of the Unthinkable.*

"changes that used . . .": Hayes and Malone, "The Ten-Year Century."

## **PROLOGUE:** PARTY LIKE IT'S 1999

"Times Square 2000 . . .": McFadden, "1/1/00: From Bali to Broadway."

## **2000:** RED AMERICA, BLUE AMERICA

The general feeling . . . country: Pew Research Center, "Optimism Reigns, Technology Plays Key Role."

"Never before has . . .": Clinton, "Address before a Joint Session."

"compassionate conservative" and "a different kind . . .": Bruni, "Bush's Tune Is the Same Even as the Pitch Varies."

"I don't think . . .": Commission on Presidential Debates, "The Second Gore-Bush Presidential Debate."

"When will the . . .": Willoughby, "Burning Up."

"In retrospect, it . . .": Lewis, *Panic*, 159.

A week after . . .: Gibbs, "Campaign 2000."

“Let me make . . .” and “Your younger brother . . .”: Duffy, “Election 2000.”

“a uniter”: Horowitz, “I’m a Uniter, Not a Divider.”

### **2001:** JANUARY TO SEPTEMBER

“Hail to the...”: Rosenbaum, “The Inauguration: The Demonstrations.”

“military committee”: *The 9/11 Commission Report*, 109.

“We do not . . .”: bin Laden, “Fatwa Urging Jihad against Americans.”

“Bin Laden determined . . .”: *The 9/11 Commission Report*, 261.

“terrorist factory”: *The 9/11 Commission Report*, 233.

### **2001:** SEPTEMBER TO DECEMBER

“We have some . . .”: *The 9/11 Commission Report*, 6.

“Somebody’s going to . . .”: *The 9/11 Commission Report*, 39.

“We will make . . .”: *The 9/11 Commission Report*, 326.

“*Nous sommes tous* . . .”: Colombani, “Nous sommes tous Américains.”

“The enemy of . . . defeated”: *The 9/11 Commission Report*, 337.

### **2002:** AN AXIS OF EVIL

“At this moment . . .”: Woodward, “A Course of Confident Action.”

“the global war on . . .”: Bush, “President Delivers ‘State of the Union.’”

“Our cause is . . .”: Bush, “President Delivers ‘State of the Union.’”

“The war on . . .”: Woodward, *Plan of Attack*, 112.

“You are going . . .”: Woodward, *Plan of Attack*, 150.

"There is no . . .": Woodward, *Plan of Attack*, 164.

"U.S. Says Hussein . . .": Gordon, "Threats and Responses."

"We don't want . . .": Woodward, *Plan of Attack*, 179.

"there is a . . .": Woodward, "A Course of Confident Action."

"The Iraqi regime . . .": Woodward, *Plan of Attack*, 150.

Polls showed a majority . . . and "personally involved": Feldmann, "The Impact of Bush Linking 9/11 and Iraq."

A top CIA . . .: Woodward, *Plan of Attack*, 107.

A 2000 report from . . .: Woodward, *Plan of Attack*, 194.

"We judge that . . .": National Foreign Intelligence Board. *National Intelligence Estimate*, 5.

"We have to . . .": Gilmore, *Frontline*, "The Dark Side."

"This was a . . .": Gilmore, *Frontline*, "The Torture Question."

## **2003:** MISSION ACCOMPLISHED

"greeted as liberators": Ricks, *Fiasco*, 98.

"will help eliminate . . .": Duffy, "A Question of Trust."

"Stuff happens. Freedom's . . .": Ricks, *Fiasco*, 136.

"major combat operations . . .": Rhem, "President Bush Proclaims End to Major Combat Ops in Iraq."

"We flew on . . .": Gilmore, *Frontline*, "The Lost Year in Iraq."

"There are some . . .": Ricks, *Fiasco*, 172.

a former ambassador . . . : Wilson, "What I Didn't Find in Africa."

"I am with . . .": Shane, "Inside a 9/11 Mastermind's Interrogation."

"We got him.": Ricks, *Fiasco*, 262.

## 2004: TRUTHINESS

"Atrocities" and "for a mistake": United States Senate, Committee on Foreign Relations.

"I don't think . . .": "Testimony of David Kay."

In January, a poll . . .: Pew Research Center, "Iraq Prison Scandal Hits Home, But Most Reject Troop Pullout."

Kerry's heroism in Vietnam . . .: Frank, "Campaign '04."

"We're not talking . . .": Colbert, *The Colbert Report.*

"Truthiness is tearing . . .": Rabin, "Interview: Stephen Colbert."

## 2005: A DELUGE OF PROBLEMS

"I want this . . .": Safire, "Bush's 'Freedom Speech.'"

"The survival of liberty . . .": Bush, "Second Inaugural Address."

"on the march": CNN.com, "Bush: Freedom on the March."

"the pygmy": Sanger, *The Inheritance*, 302.

"disgraceful stain . . .": Richter, "Tehran's Genocidal Incitement against Israel."

"If a TV . . .": Rohde, "How a 'Good War' in Afghanistan Went Bad."

"They're not sure . . .": Sanger, *The Inheritance*, 155.

"Brownie, you're doing . . .": White House Office of the Press Secretary. "President Arrives in Alabama, Briefed on Hurricane Katrina."

## 2006: YOU HAVE SIX BILLION FRIEND REQUESTS

"just setting up . . .": Dorsey, Twitter status, @Jack.

"Let's give a . . .": Craig, "Allen Quip Provokes Outrage, Apology."

"I hear the . . .": CNN.com, "Bush: 'I'm the Decider' on Rumsfeld."

"If we give . . .": CNN.com transcripts, "American Morning."

"the Iraq war . . .": Mazzetti, "Spy Agencies Say Iraq War Worsens Terrorism Threat."

By March 2006 . . . and "Until now, the . . .": Pew Research Center survey reports, "Bush Approval Falls to 33%, Congress Earns Rare Praise."

"banker to the...": Yunus, *Banker to the Poor.*

"Lasting peace cannot . . .": Nobel Committee Statement, 2006.

## **2007:** DOUBLE DOWN

"Absolutely, we're winning.": Ricks, *The Gamble*, 58.

"Cheney looked like . . .": Sanger, *The Inheritance*, 329.

"While 84% of . . .": Pew Research Center, "Public Praises Science."

"We do not . . .": Kluger, "What Now for Our Feverish Planet?"

"If the attacks . . .": Ricks, *Fiasco*, 172.

"In Afghanistan we . . .": Sanger, *The Inheritance*, 119.

## **2008:** CHANGE HAS COME

"in no other . . .": Obama, "A More Perfect Union."

"Dick Cheney and . . .": Tumulty, "Barack Obama: The Contender."

"Making change is . . .": Carlson, "Hillary Tries Temper, Tears to Stop Obama."

"Who's Palin?": Thomas, "How He Did It."

A writer in . . .: Cassidy, "The Next Crash."

"The American home . . .": Tully, "Is This House Worth $1.2 Million?"

"The fundamentals of . . ." and "It's not that . . .": Thomas, "How He Did It."

"I am just . . .": Thomas, "How He Did It."

" an Arab": Nicolas, "McCain Moves to Calm His Backers."

"It has been . . .": Thomas, "How He Did It."

## **2009:** IS COMPROMISE A DIRTY WORD?

"I think that . . .": Balz, "From the Start, Putting a Bold Stamp on the White House."

"Now, there are . . .": Obama, "President Barack Obama's Inaugural Address."

"Obviously, at the . . .": Stolberg, "Obama Is Nudging Views on Race, a Survey Finds."

"Although I believe . . .": Obama, "The President's Speech in Cairo."

Protestors marching on . . .: Thrush, "Jewish Dems Denounce Tea Party Signs."

"You lie!": Hulse, "In Lawmaker's Outburst, a Rare Breach of Protocol."

# BIBLIOGRAPHY


Balz, Dan. "From the Start, Putting a Bold Stamp on the White House." *Washington Post*, April 29, 2009.

Becker, Jasper. *The Chinese*. New York: The Free Press, 2000.

bin Laden, Osama, and al Qaeda, "Fatwa Urging Jihad against Americans." Published by *Al-Quds al-'Arabi*, London, February 23, 1998.

Bruni, Frank. "Bush's Tune Is the Same Even as the Pitch Varies." *New York Times*, September 16, 2000.

Bush, George W. "President Delivers 'State of the Union.'" http://georgewbush-whitehouse.archives.gov/news/releases/2003/01/20030128-19.html, January 28, 2003.

Bush, George W. Second Inaugural Address, January 20, 2005. http://georgewbush-whitehouse.archives.gov/news/releases/2005/01/20050120-1.html.

Carlson, Margaret. "Hillary Tries Temper, Tears to Stop Obama." *Bloomberg*, January 8, 2008. http://www.bloomberg.com/apps/news?pid=20601039&sid=a7MTl5pj764g&refer=home.

Cassidy, John. "The Next Crash." *The New Yorker*, November 11, 2002.

Clinton, William J. "Address Before a Joint Session of the Congress on the State of the Union, January 27, 2000." The American Presidency Project, University of California-Santa Barbara. http://www.presidency.ucsb.edu/ws/index.php?pid=58708.

Commission on Presidential Debates. "The Second Gore-Bush Presidential Debate," October 11, 2000. http://www.debates.org/index.php?page=october-11-2000-debate-transcript.

CNN.com. "Bush: Freedom on the March," March 5, 2005. http://www.cnn.com/2005/ALLPOLITICS/03/05/bush.radio/.

CNN.com. "Bush: 'I'm the 'Decider' on Rumsfeld," April 18, 2006. http://www.cnn.com/2006/POLITICS/04/18/rumsfeld/.

CNN.com transcripts. "American Morning," September 5, 2006. http://transcripts.cnn.com/TRANSCRIPTS/0609/05/ltm.03.html.

Colbert, Stephen, producer. *The Colbert Report*, October 17, 2005. http://www.colbertnation.com/the-colbert-report-videos/24039/october-17-2005/the-word---truthiness.

Coll, Steve. *Ghost Wars*. New York: Penguin, 2004.

Colombani, Jean-Marie. "Nous sommes tous Américains." *Le Monde*, September 13, 2001.

Craig, Tim, and Michael D. Shear. "Allen Quip Provokes Outrage, Apology." *Washington Post*, August 15, 2006.

Dionne, E. J. *Why Americans Hate Politics*. New York: Touchstone, 1991.

Dorsey, Jack. Twitter status, @Jack, March 21, 2006. http://twitter.com/jack/status/20.

Duffy, Michael, with James Carney, John F. Dickerson, Tamala M. Edwards, and Karen Tumulty. "Election 2000: What It Took." *Time*, November 20, 2000.

Duffy, Michael, and James Carney. "A Question of Trust." *Time*, July 21, 2003.

Feldmann, Linda. "The Impact of Bush Linking 9/11 and Iraq." *Christian Science Monitor*, March 14, 2003.

Ferguson, Niall. "The Axis of Upheaval." *Foreign Policy*, March/April 2009.

Frank, Mitch. "Campaign '04: Kerry in Combat: Setting the Record Straight." *Time*, August 30, 2004.

Friedman, Thomas L. *The World Is Flat: A Brief History of the Twenty-first Century*. New York: Picador, 2007.

Ghosh, Aparisim. "People Who Mattered: Iraqi Citizens; What Civil War Has Done to a Family." *Time*, December 25, 2006.

Gibbs, Nancy, with James Carney, Tamala M. Edwards, John F. Dickerson, Michael Duffy, and Eric Pooley. "Campaign 2000: How Bush Lost His Edge." *Time*, September 18, 2000.

Gilmore, Jim, and Michael Kirk, producers. *Frontline*, "The Dark Side." A production of WGBH Boston for PBS, 2006.
http://www.pbs.org/wgbh/pages/frontline/darkside/.

Gilmore, Jim, and Michael Kirk, producers. *Frontline*. "The Lost Year in Iraq." A production of WGBH Boston for PBS, 2005.
http://www.pbs.org/wgbh/pages/frontline/yeariniraq/.

Gilmore, Jim, and Michael Kirk, producers. *Frontline*,"The Torture Question." A production of WGBH Boston for PBS, 2005.
http://www.pbs.org/wgbh/pages/frontline/torture/.

Gordon, Michael R., and Judith Miller. "Threats and Responses: The Iraqis: U.S. Says Hussein Intensifies Quest for A-Bomb Parts." *New York Times*, September 8, 2002.

Hayes, Tom, and Michael S. Malone. "The Ten-Year Century." *Wall Street Journal*, August 10, 2009.

Hersh, Seymour. "Torture at Abu Ghraib." *The New Yorker*, May 10, 2004.

Horowitz, David. "I'm a Uniter, not a Divider." *Salon*, May 6, 1999.

Hulse, Carl. "In Lawmaker's Outburst, a Rare Breach of Protocol." *New York Times*, September 9, 2009.

Kluger, Jeffrey. "What Now for Our Feverish Planet?" *Time*, March 29, 2007.

Lewis, Michael, ed. *Panic: The Story of Modern Financial Insanity.* New York: Norton, 2009.

Luce, Edward. *In Spite of the Gods: The Strange Rise of Modern India.* New York: Doubleday, 2007.

McFadden, Robert D. "1/1/00: From Bali to Broadway." *New York Times*, January 1, 2000.

Manjoo, Farhad. *True Enough: Learning to Live in a Post-Fact Society.* Hoboken, N.J.: Wiley, 2008.

Mazzetti, Mark. "Spy Agencies Say Iraq War Worsens Terrorism Threat." *New York Times*, September 24, 2006.

National Foreign Intelligence Board. *National Intelligence Estimate: Iraq's Continuing Programs for Weapons of Mass Destruction.* October 2002.

National Intelligence Council. *Global Trends 2025: A Transformed World.* November 2008.

Nicolas, Peter, and Seema Mehta. "McCain Moves to Calm His Backers." *Los Angeles Times*, October 11, 2008.

*The 9/11 Commission Report: Final Report of the National Commission on Terrorist Attacks upon the United States.* New York: Norton, 2004.

Nobel Committee Statement, 2006. http://nobelprize.org/nobel_prizes/peace/laureates/2006/press.html.

Obama, Barack. *Dreams from My Father.* New York: Three Rivers Press, 1995.

Obama, Barack. "A More Perfect Union." Speech transcript, *New York Times*, March 18, 2008.

Obama, Barack. "President Barack Obama's Inaugural Address," January 21, 2009. http://www.whitehouse.gov/video/President-Barack-Obamas-Inaugural-Address-January-20-2009.

Obama, Barack. "The President's Speech in Cairo: A New Beginning," June 4, 2009. http://www.whitehouse.gov/blog/NewBeginning.

Pew Research Center for the People & the Press. "Bush Approval Falls to 33%, Congress Earns Rare Praise." *Survey Reports*, March 15, 2006.

Pew Research Center for the People & the Press. "Iraq Prison Scandal Hits Home, But Most Reject Troop Pullout." *Survey Reports*, May 12, 2004.

Pew Research Center for the People & the Press. "Optimism Reigns, Technology Plays Key Role." *Survey Reports*, October 24, 1999.

Pew Research Center for the People & the Press. "Public Praises Science; Scientists Fault Public, Media." *Survey Reports*, July 9, 2009.

Pollack, Kenneth M. *The Persian Puzzle: The Conflict between Iran and America*. New York: Random House, 2004.

Rabin, Nathan. "Interview: Stephen Colbert." *A.V. Club*, January 26, 2006.

Ramo, Joshua Cooper. *The Age of the Unthinkable*. New York: Little, Brown and Company, 2009.

Rashid, Ahmed. *Descent into Chaos*. New York: Viking, 2008.

Rhem, Kathleen T. "President Bush Proclaims End to Major Combat Ops in Iraq." *American Forces Press Service*, May 1, 2003.

Richter, Elihu D., and Alex Barnea. "Tehran's Genocidal Incitement against Israel." *Middle East Quarterly*, Summer 2009.

Ricks, Thomas E. *Fiasco*. New York: Penguin, 2006.

Ricks, Thomas E. *The Gamble*. New York: Penguin, 2009.

Rohde, David, and David E. Sanger. "How a 'Good War' in Afghanistan Went Bad." *New York Times*, August 12, 2007.

Rosenbaum, David. "The Inauguration: The Demonstrations: Protesters in the Thousands Sound Off in the Capital." *New York Times*, January 21, 2001.

Safire, William. "Bush's 'Freedom Speech.'" *New York Times*, January 21, 2005.

Sanger, David E. *The Inheritance: The World Obama Confronts and the Challenges to American Power*. New York: Harmony Books, 2009

Shane, Scott. "Inside a 9/11 Mastermind's Interrogation." *New York Times*, June 22, 2008.

Stewart, James B. "Eight Days: The Battle to Save the American Financial System." *The New Yorker*, September 21, 2009.

Stolberg, Sheryl Gay, and Marjorie Connelly. "Obama Is Nudging Views on Race, a Survey Finds." *New York Times*, April 27, 2009.

"Testimony of David Kay before the Senate Armed Services Committee." January 28, 2004. Federal News Service. Reprinted by George Washington University, National Security Archive. http://www.gwu.edu/~nsarchiv/NSAEBB/NSAEBB80/kaytestimony.pdf.

Thomas, Evan. "How He Did It." *Newsweek*, November 6, 2008.

Thrush, Glenn. "Jewish Dems Denounce Tea Party Signs." *Politico*, November 5, 2009.

Tully, Shawn. "Is This House Worth $1.2 Million?" *Fortune*, October 28, 2002.

Tumulty, Karen. "Barack Obama: The Contender." *Time*, November 29, 2007.

United States Senate, Committee on Foreign Relations, Legislative Proposals Relating to the War in Southeast Asia Thursday, April 22, 1971, Washington, D.C. http://www.c-span.org/vote2004/jkerrytestimony.asp.

White House Office of the Press Secretary. "President Arrives in Alabama, Briefed on Hurricane Katrina," September 2, 2005. http://georgewbush-whitehouse.archives.gov/news/releases/2005/09/images/20050902-2_f1g5125-515h.html.

Willoughby, Jack. "Burning Up." *Barron's*, March 20, 2000.

Wilson, Joseph. "What I Didn't Find in Africa." *New York Times*, July 6, 2003.

Woodward, Bob. "A Course of Confident Action." *Washington Post*, November 19, 2002.

Woodward, Bob. *Plan of Attack*. New York: Simon & Schuster, 2004.

Yunus, Muhammad. *Banker to the Poor*. New York, Public Affairs, 2003.

# INDEX

Note: Page numbers in *italics* refer to illustrations or captions.
Page numbers followed by a *t* refer to text boxes.

# ACKNOWLEDGMENTS

This book began as a conversation between my gifted editor, Catherine Frank, and me. She said, "Why don't you explain to young readers . . . all this . . . this past decade?" So this book is her fault. But, without her patience, determination, and intelligence, I would not be holding a labor I am immensely proud of.

Thanks also to the other great people at Viking who made this happen—Jim Hoover, Janet Pascal, and Regina Hayes.

I've tried to give a snapshot of the last ten years, and it wouldn't have been possible without the in-depth portraits by talented journalists who covered the past decade firsthand, particularly Steve Coll, Peter Bergen, Thomas Ricks, David Sanger, John Dickerson, and Karen Tumulty. I also must thank some kind friends in Kentucky and Scotland who gave moral support. And finally, thanks to my dog Boudreaux—who always knew when I needed a hug.

EAST ORANGE PUBLIC LIBRARY
3 2665 0041 4884 9